M

HIDY OCHIAI'S
COMPLETE BOOK OF
SELF-DEFENSE
∎∎∎

HIDY OCHIAI'S
COMPLETE BOOK OF SELF-DEFENSE
▪▪▪
HIDY OCHIAI

CB
CONTEMPORARY BOOKS

Library of Congress Cataloging-in-Publication Data

Ochiai, Hidy.
    [Complete book of self-defense]
    Hidy Ochiai's complete book of self-defense / Hidy Ochiai.
        p.   cm.
    Includes index.
    ISBN 0-8092-4055-6
    1. Hand-to-hand fighting, Oriental.   2. Karate.   I. Title.
II. Title: Complete book of self-defense.
GV1112.027   1991
796.8'15—dc20   90-19279
                                                                      CIP

All photos by Tony Frontera.

Chapter 9, "Karate and the Martial Arts: A Philosophy," was
previously published as Chapter 6, "Philosophy of Karate,"
in *Hidy Ochiai's Living Karate* by Hidy Ochiai, Chicago:
Contemporary Books, Inc., 1986. Reprinted by permission.

Published by Contemporary Books
An imprint of NTC/Contemporary Publishing Company
4255 West Touhy Avenue, Lincolnwood, Illinois 60646-1975
Manufactured in the United States of America
International Standard Book Number: 0-8092-4055-6
20   19   18   17   16   15   14   13   12   11   10   9   8

Contents

Preface

It would be wonderful to live in a society in which the need for self-defense did not exist—to dwell in cities and towns whose citizens were mutually respectful, considerate, and trusting.

The sad reality, however, is that we cannot expect all people to be good and kind to one another. Society perenially suffers people who are violent and lawless and who threaten innocent citizens striving to live in peace. On a larger scale, there are threats of direct confrontations all the time.

But are we to roll over and simply accept violence as a natural evil of humanity and society? No! Even if we cannot control the major forms of violence such as war, we *can* take steps to minimize the violence in our immediate surroundings—and to learn to defend ourselves until the day comes when citizens can walk the streets without fear. Even a pacifist should know how to avoid being hurt unnecessarily by a violent person.

We must begin by understanding that violent individuals often lack self-esteem and a sense of security. Compare such people to confident men and women, who do not easily resort to violence to solve their problems. By properly educating young children to respect themselves and others, we can certainly help to eliminate some of the roots of violent behavior.

The martial arts provide an excellent vehicle not only to defend yourself against the violent individuals who yet plague us, but also to instill self-confidence and self-respect. As you study the art of self-defense, you will see that its mental aspect is just as important as, if not more important than, its physical techniques. You must try, therefore, to increase your mental strength through self-control,

self-discipline, concentration, confidence, and respect for yourself and others. A good teacher of the martial arts can guide his or her students in attaining these mental qualities in training, but if you practice alone, you must work to develop them on your own.

Good mental health combines with physical fitness to help you become more proficient in your physical skills, and physical fitness further improves your mental abilities. Clearly, the execution of acquired techniques is more effective if you are in proper physical condition than if you are not. And as you recognize the crucial role your mind plays in self-defense and continue to train with sincerity, you will naturally begin to feel increased confidence, alertness, patience, and inner strength as you become more proficient in your physical skills.

Sound physical and mental well-being will allow you to cope with all kinds of predicaments more resourcefully. By acquiring inner peace, self-confidence, and respect for yourself and others, you will actually come to avoid physical confrontations whenever possible and to detest violence. Thus, the art of self-defense is not only a practical tool for people who wish to take care of themselves if they are attacked or threatened, but also a vehicle to educate young and old people in more positive living.

This book should serve those who wish to study karate but do not have the opportunity to attend a school of martial arts. The volume is also intended for students who wish to review and augment their knowledge of the martial arts. It should prove particularly useful as a textbook for a mini self-defense course or for the basic karate classes in colleges,

YMCAs, YWCAs, and community programs.

If you intend to practice the techniques in this book by yourself, try to use the concept of the "imaginary opponent" when practicing. You can make considerable progress training alone if you follow the book's instructions carefully. If you practice with actual partners, please make safety a top priority—for your own well-being and theirs. All techniques should be executed with 100 percent control by holding your movement back one to three inches from your targets, depending on your proficiency.

No book, of course, can replace instruction by teachers trained in the martial arts, and I encourage you to attend courses when you can. Although training under a professional takes a tremendous amount of dedication, time, and effort, your rewards will be great. Compared with self-training, your work with a professional teacher will allow you to learn the *vital*, not just the mere, elements of self-defense; to develop finer physical skills; to practice techniques for *art's* sake; and, overall, to become a more proficient martial artist. The confidence you develop will enhance your entire life.

HIDY OCHIAI'S
COMPLETE BOOK OF
SELF-DEFENSE
...

1 Introduction

No one can become truly proficient in the art of self-defense by learning only physical techniques. In a very simple case, such as someone's grabbing your arm against your will, you may be able to defend yourself without much mental strength. But more complex situations require a keen mind and inner fortitude. Take this story of a Japanese tea master and a samurai as an example.

A famous tea master of seventeenth-century Japan once insulted a low-positioned samurai by accident. The tea master profusely apologized to the samurai, but the samurai adamantly refused to accept the humble apology. Instead, the samurai demanded that they duel to settle the matter.

The tea master did not know what to do, for he was a man of peace and was not accustomed to fighting. He did not even carry a sword. The samurai, on the other hand, was interested only in fighting and demonstrating his skill in sword fighting. The tea master was finally forced to accept the challenge by the samurai. And so on the day before the duel, the tea master held a sword for the first time, and someone showed him how to swing it.

Although not familiar with the way of the sword, the tea master was a Zen master as well, and had so cultivated his mind that he was not afraid of death. Before the duel, he meditated in a sitting position for a while, then made tea, which he drank ceremoniously as he always had. His mind was calm and stable.

People gathering for the duel were amazed at the tea master's appearance. The meek-looking man was gone. There stood a man full of pride and confidence. The tea master showed no fear of death. He knew he was right in the eyes of heaven (the gods), and he believed that he could not be defeated by the ill-willed samurai. The tea master's confidence and belief in the self shone in his eyes.

The samurai, as soon as he saw the tea master standing proudly and calmly with the sword in his hands, realized that he had challenged the wrong man. He called off the duel and ran away.

This story, of course, illustrates how strength of mind and belief in yourself help prepare you for fighting—and can even overcome a violent situation. Indeed, physical skills are nothing unless they are properly utilized when needed, and only mental strength makes that possible. Mental strength includes self-discipline, self-control, confidence, and respect for yourself and others. A greater ability to concentrate also comes with serious practice.

Simple self-defense techniques can be drawn from "real-life" situations and from lessons in such traditional martial arts as karate, judo, and aikido. Striking a would-be mugger with a handbag is a technique in self-defense. Jabbing an attacker's rib cage with a key chain can be an effective self-defense technique, too. In this sense, self-defense techniques are not really difficult to learn. Commonsense approaches can work in many cases, and "mental" self-defense often proves to be more important than physical technique. Traditional martial arts strengthen your physical and mental self-defense.

However, no matter how many situational self-defense techniques you learn, they can never cover all of the situations that can occur on the streets or anywhere else. This is the reason it is important to practice prearranged techniques, which are akin to grammar in language, with intensity. Just as you learn to apply grammar rules naturally in all your communication, so you must become able to apply prearranged techniques to any situation at will. Correct application makes the "grammars" become alive and useful.

Needless to say, it is neither practical nor wise to seek opportunities to apply the grammar of self-defense on the streets. That would be looking for trouble, and it is not in accordance with the principle of the art of self-defense.

The true student of the art of self-defense *never* looks for trouble but uses the techniques only to defend him- or herself. We all must obey and respect law enforcement officials when they are carrying out their public duties. Even when you are defending yourself, if law enforcement officials are available in time, you should leave the situation to them as much as possible. In this book, therefore, *references to self-defense situations mean situations in which you have no other recourse but your own ability to defend yourself.*

In addition to improving your physical condition, practicing prearranged techniques helps to develop confidence as you become more aware of your potential range of physical strength and control. True confidence thus acquired makes you calmer, more peaceful, and, consequently, less belligerent. It also enables you to avoid potential trouble without fear or panic. Proper training in the art of self-defense can even make a violent person less brutal.

The attainment of proficiency in any art or sport requires perseverance and constant effort, and the art of self-defense is no exception. Therefore, if you seriously practice the art on a regular basis, you naturally develop self-discipline and patience, which you can apply to job performance, academic work, sports, and arts.

To make your techniques more effective, you must utilize *ki-ai*. Some people think ki-ai is merely shouting or yelling to produce stronger power from within and to make the techniques more effective. But this opinion misrepresents ki-ai. Let's look first at the phrase's meaning. The *ki* of ki-ai is a Japanese word that describes such things as spirit, mind, heart, mood, care, air, and atmosphere; in terms of the martial arts *ki* specifically connotes a certain invisible quality that harmonizes mind and body for the maximum effectiveness of the techniques. The *ai* of ki-ai denotes the meeting and coordinating of timing. Thus, the focus and power of the techniques in the martial arts are enhanced by usage of ki-ai.

As I have noted in my earlier books, executing a technique with a proper ki-ai is akin to utilizing all available weapons to attack an enemy without thinking of a second chance. Merely uttering sound is not ki-ai, and ki-ai may or may not be expressed with loud sound. The distinction between sounded and unsounded ki-ai is not really significant as long as ki-ai comes from the power that emanates from the lower abdomen (*tan-den*). When you breathe properly, using the lower abdomen, all your muscles and nerves focus on the execution of your technique. Although there is nothing mysterious about it, ki-ai produces a certain energy as well—spiritual, physical, and mental. Your physical movement becomes more effective and precise. Feelings of self-assertiveness and self-control also are enhanced. (A loud ki-ai might even scare your opponent—and thus increase your courage to do what you feel is necessary.)

According to Miyamoto Musashi, a great samurai who died in 1645, there should be no distinction between techniques taught to an experienced person and an inexperienced one. The purpose of combats is to win, which means that one must defeat the opponent. Applying Musashi's theory, there should not be such things as advanced or basic self-defense techniques. If you are forced to defend yourself, it is nonsensical to debate whether you should use the advanced techniques or the beginner's techniques. You must defend yourself, no matter what. Categorizing the techniques is absurd in a real self-defense situation.

However, there *are* some techniques that are more approachable by novice students than others, and techniques *can* be categorized according to different levels of ability in students. For example, a person who is not agile initially may have difficulty executing a roundhouse kick or a side kick. We must recognize a certain effective order of learning, from a beginning stage to an advanced level.

This book is intended to help those who wish to study the art of self-defense from various aspects, practical and traditional. It emphasizes physical fitness as well as mental conditioning, for the basis of real self-defense techniques lies in the total well-being of the practitioner. Ultimately, as you continue to study the art of self-defense diligently, you come to realize the absurdity of violent behavior in a civilized society and detest violence without fearing it—which may be a sign that you have become an advanced student in the art of self-defense.

An advanced student may try to walk away from trouble or potential trouble, for that is an "advanced" technique. However, if you are forced to defend yourself with no chance of walking or running away from the situation, you must do so with all your strength, mental, physical, and spiritual. This book shows you how.

MASTERY OF THE SELF

Diligent training allows one not only to become technically proficient in arts and sports, but also to gain self-mastery. Proper training—learning correct forms and practicing carefully over many years—should automatically increase one's capacity for self-discipline and self-control. It is important to apply these precious qualities of mind to further develop oneself in one's work. And it is vital to take responsibility for the consequence of one's behavior. To become a master of an art is a fine thing, and to become an expert of craft is a great achievement in any person's life. But it is more important to become the master of the self— to exert control over oneself in life.

A great threat to our pursuit of mastery of the self is artificial stimuli such as drugs and alcohol. Some people claim they have experimented with drugs to expand self-awareness and gain insight into life. But by accepting drugs one surrenders the center of the self, that is, relinquishes self-mastery and self-respect. Drugs may give an illusion of well-being (hallucination), but they have nothing to do with the reality of which we are a part. A human being is equipped with whatever is needed to be greater. The greatness comes only from within the self as a result of training and discipline.

For the sake of attaining more wisdom or insight into life, it is fine if one wishes to become involved in religion. Karate is not, however, a religion. It should not become a cult, either. Karate is a "tool" to strengthen one's belief and to develop one's potential in many ways, providing the source of energy and an outlet to live a constructive life.

2 Simple Self-Defense Techniques

The techniques described in this chapter are relatively easy to learn with little technical knowledge of martial arts. These techniques are useful in "minor," one-on-one self-defense situations in which no weapons are involved and the attacker is not usually very aggressive.

It is important that you follow each technique step by step, and if an instructor is available, ask him or her to demonstrate it before you practice it. Be patient and cautious in practice. Approach the techniques as "grammars" of self-defense, which they are. As you become familiar with each technique, you may increase your speed of execution or try to practice it from a walking position rather than a static one.

Some of the techniques shown here are very useful in situations in which an acquaintance suddenly attacks you. For instance, a simple and firm technique may discourage a date who has suddenly become violent. Similarly, you can use techniques to offset aggressive actions by family members or friends.

Don't be deceived by the apparent simplicity of these techniques. A few practice sessions may give you the impression of familiarity quickly. But only careful and long practice will allow you to learn the vital points of the techniques—and to execute them at will.

SHOULDER THROW AGAINST THE ONE-ARM CHOKE

1. Your opponent chokes you from behind with his right arm. Grab the choking arm with your right hand as you tuck your chin down tightly.

2. Bring your right foot inside the opponent's right foot and lift the left arm for a back-elbow strike.

3. Execute the back-elbow strike with your left arm as you pull back your left foot so that it is closer to the opponent's left foot.

4. Squat as you pull the opponent forward slightly and place your opened left hand inside the opponent's left knee for support.

5. As you spring up with the knees and pull down the opponent's right arm, throw the opponent over your right shoulder.

6. Do not throw over your head, but over your back and right shoulder.

7. In practice, safety is the most important priority. For this reason, keep holding the opponent's right arm as you finish the throw.

8. In a real situation, holding the opponent's arm as you finish the throw gives you a better opportunity to execute a finishing technique.

OUTER MAJOR SWEEP

1. Block or parry the upper punch or the grabbing arm with your right hand.

2. Grab the attacking arm with your left hand, and push it down and inward. At the same time, strike and push the opponent's chin with the heel of your right palm.

3. Bring your left foot outside and next to the opponent's right foot.

4. Sweep the opponent's right leg with your right leg as you push his chin with your right hand and keep holding his left arm.

5. Synchronize the sweeping motion with the leg and pushing motion of the hand to make the throwing technique smooth and effective.

SELF-DEFENSE FROM A CHAIR: METHOD A

1. As you sit on a chair, someone is choking you or grabbing you from behind.

2. Bring your right foot back slightly so that it's closer to the opponent. Feel power in your lower abdomen.

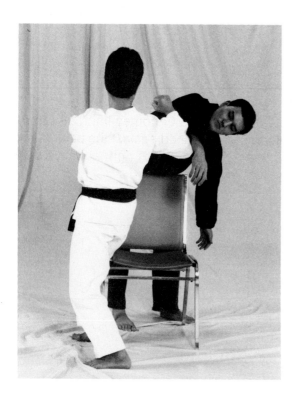

3. Move your left foot to make it line up with the right foot. At the same time, spring up your knees with ki-ai, simultaneously parrying the opponent's choking arm from your neck.

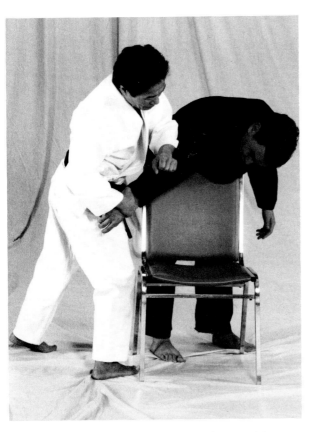

4. Grab the opponent's right arm, and immediately press on his elbow with your left forearm.

5. Keep pressing the back of the opponent's right elbow until he becomes immobilized as his abdomen is pushed against the back of the chair. Keep the opponent's right arm on top of your right thigh.

SELF-DEFENSE FROM A CHAIR: METHOD B

1. As you sit side by side with someone, he starts to put his left arm around your neck against your will. You realize that you must defend yourself against the opponent.

2. With your right elbow, execute the hard side-elbow strike to the opponent's ribs.

3. Grab the opponent's left arm (the one placed around your neck).

4. Bring the opponent's left arm over your head to the front.

5. With your right forearm, start to press on the back of the opponent's left elbow.

6. For complete submission, get off the chair and get on your right knee as you continue to press on the back of his left elbow. Place the opponent's left arm on your left knee as you execute the submission.

SELF-DEFENSE FROM A CHAIR: METHOD C

1. You are sitting side by side with someone.

2. Suddenly, the person starts to act aggressively. He puts his arm around your neck and holds your right hand.

3. First, bring your head under the opponent's left arm as you place your left thumb at the back of the opponent's right hand.

4. Keep holding the opponent's right hand, twisting it on the wrist.

5. With both hands, twist the opponent's right wrist and immobilize him.

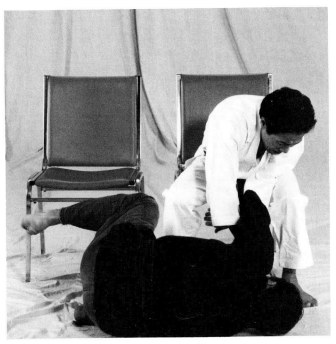

6. Keep twisting the right wrist until the opponent falls on the floor.

BEAR-HUG HOLD FROM THE FRONT: METHOD A

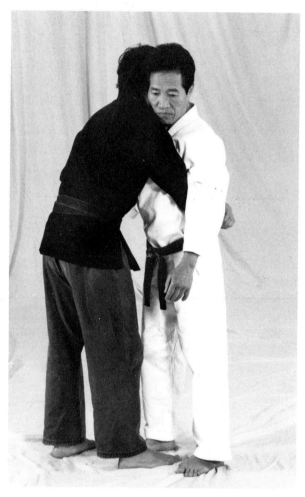

1. You are being held from the front in a bear hug, but your arms are free.

2. With your right elbow, execute a strong front-elbow strike to the opponent's left temple.

3. Follow the front-elbow strike with a front-knee kick to the opponent's abdomen.

4. With the edge of your right foot, execute a strong stamping kick to the opponent's right instep.

5. Bring your right leg outside of the opponent's right leg and prepare for the outer major sweep.

BEAR-HUG HOLD FROM THE FRONT: METHOD B

1. You are being attacked from the front with a bear-hug hold over the arms.

2. First, attack the opponent with a front-knee kick to his groin or lower stomach to weaken or "freeze" him.

3. At the moment when the opponent "freezes" because of your front-knee kick, quickly spin under the opponent's right arm to come outside of the opponent's right foot.

4. From this position, you are now ready to escape or attempt to overcome the opponent.

5. To bring about his submission, place your left forearm on the back of the opponent's right elbow.

6. Press on the opponent's right elbow with your left forearm as you squat. Make sure that the opponent's right hand is placed on your right thigh.

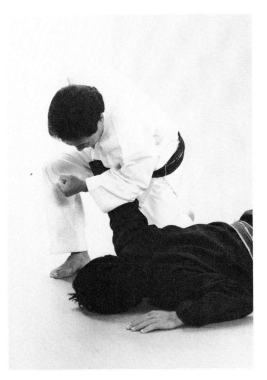

7. Get on your left knee and complete the submission. Make sure that you are pressing on the back of the opponent's right elbow.

BEAR-HUG HOLD FROM BEHIND

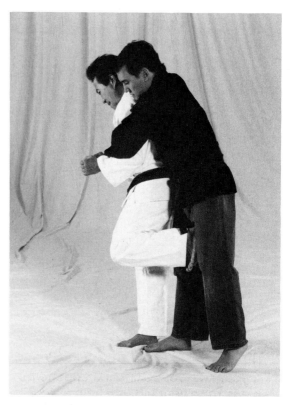

1. Your opponent attacks you from behind with a bear-hug hold.

2. Execute a back kick to the opponent's leg or groin. The kick will momentarily weaken the opponent's hold.

3. Immediately move your right foot so that it is outside the opponent's right foot.

4. Bring your left foot behind the opponent's right leg and raise your left arm high to free it from the opponent's hold.

5. Push the opponent backward over your left thigh. To do this, push the opponent with your left arm and press the opponent's right leg with your left knee from behind.

6. The finishing technique, if needed, can be a kick or a punch. The important thing is to keep your balance at the moment you are throwing so that you can execute any technique against the opponent.

ONE-ARM CHOKE FROM BEHIND

1. Your opponent grabs your neck with his left arm and holds your right hand with his right hand.

2. To remove his right hand, twist your right hand against its thumb. As you take control of his right hand, bring your head under the opponent's left arm.

3. With both hands, hold the opponent's right hand. The thumbs of both hands meet at the back of his right hand. To further weaken the opponent, execute the front-knee kick to the opponent's midsection.

4. Take the opponent down on his back by pressing his right wrist with both your hands.

5. As the opponent falls backward, release your hands from his right hand. (Depending on the situation, you may or may not need to execute a further technique.)

UPPER ATTACK FROM SIDE: METHOD A

1. Block the opponent's attack with your left arm.

2. Slide in to get close to the opponent, and execute the left-elbow strike to his midsection.

3. Bring your left hand in front of the opponent's shoulder, simultaneously sliding your left foot closer to the opponent's right knee. (Your left knee makes contact with the back of the opponent's right knee.)

4. By pushing your left arm backward against the opponent's left shoulder and by pushing your left knee against the opponent's knee from behind, throw the opponent on his back.

UPPER ATTACK FROM SIDE: METHOD B

1. Block the opponent's upper attack with your right arm. (Stances can vary. In street situations, you may more likely block with the natural stance. In a practice situation, you may try to use different stances for the sake of learning.)

2. Slide in to get close to the opponent, and execute a side-elbow strike to the opponent's ribs.

3. Get down on your right knee, and grab the back of the opponent's ankle with your left hand. At the same time, use your right forearm to push the opponent's right knee from inside.

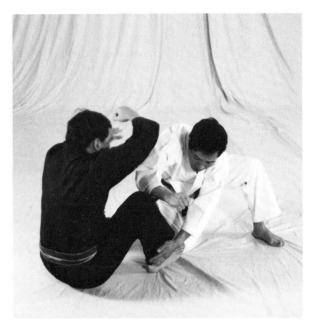

4. By pushing your right forearm against the opponent's right knee from inside, and simultaneously pulling his ankle with your left hand, throw the opponent down.

TWO-HAND CHOKING OR GRABBING FROM BEHIND: METHOD A

1. The opponent grabs you from behind with two hands.

2. Bring your right foot slightly backward.

3. Move your left foot forward, and bring both arms in front of your chest with the fists showing their palm sides inward.

4. With a sudden and strong motion, spin clockwise to parry the opponent's grabbing hands from the back of your neck.

5. Grab the opponent's arm with your right hand.

6. Execute the strong round-house knee kick to the opponent's midsection.

TWO-HAND CHOKING OR GRABBING FROM BEHIND: METHOD B

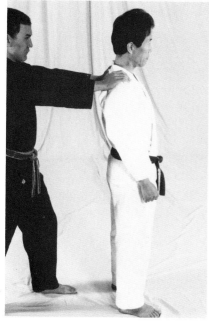  

1. As you assume a natural stance, the opponent grabs your neck from behind. (It can be interpreted as choking or grabbing.)

2. Squat halfway down as you twist your upper body to your left side.

3. Take off one of the opponent's arms. In this case, take off the left with your left arm by swinging it from underneath.

4. Keep turning to your right. At this moment, the opponent loses his grabbing power with only one hand on your neck.

5. Grab the opponent's right arm with your right hand and pull him forward.

6. With your right foot, execute a roundhouse kick to the opponent's midsection.

7. As you place your right foot on the ground after the roundhouse kick, execute the front-elbow strike to the opponent's temple area.

8. The finishing technique can be a strong back-fist strike to the opponent's face.

FULL-NELSON HOLD

1. The opponent holds you from behind with a full-nelson hold.

2. Twist your body in such a way that you can bring your right foot outside of the opponent's right foot.

3. Next bring your left foot behind the opponent's right foot, and place it between the opponents two feet.

4. Push the opponent backward with your left arm across the opponent's upper chest.

5. Shake off the opponent strongly so that he may let his arms go off from your shoulders. But keep holding on to the opponent's right hand with your right hand.

6. The finishing technique can be a kick to the opponent's head or a punch. Or you may simply walk away from him after you escape from his hold.

FROM UPPER BLOCK TO COUNTERATTACK: METHOD A

1. Suppose you execute the left upper block against the opponent's left upper punch.

2. The side kick to the knee is effective in stopping the opponent.

3. You may execute the front kick to the opponent's midsection with the ball of your foot.

4. The side-thrust kick to the opponent's midsection can be very effective.

5. You may execute the roundhouse kick to the opponent's face, although it may not be practical.

6. You may try a high hook kick to the opponent's temple with the heel.

FROM UPPER BLOCK TO COUNTERATTACK: METHOD B

1. Suppose you execute the left upper block against the opponent's left upper punch.

2. Grab the opponent's left arm, and counterattack with a right reverse punch to the opponent's midsection.

3. Pull the opponent forward and attack him with the front-elbow strike to his temple.

4. After the upper block, step forward with your left foot and immediately execute the front-elbow strike to the opponent's midsection.

5. Grab the opponent's attacking arm with your left hand and execute the right knife-hand strike to the opponent's right temple.

6. Execute the right ridge-hand strike to the opponent's left temple.

3   Ground Techniques

You may be forced to defend yourself when you are lying on your stomach or back. If at all possible, try to get up on your feet at the first opportunity. However, if you are held down by the opponent, don't panic. With the power and strength in your lower stomach, use your legs to push or throw back the opponent. Use a loud *ki-ai*, which can give you more courage and strength.

Try to keep your head up all the time you are on the ground, and keep both knees fully bent so that they can be used to offset the opponent. To throw the opponent backward or forward, and even sideward, use the scissors techniques shown on the following pages. Try to get up on your feet as soon as you throw the opponent and gain control over the situation.

Use every means possible to get away from your opponent. Don't hesitate to fight back by biting, spitting, or scratching; although these techniques are not considered part of the traditional martial arts, actual self-defense uses every available means.

PUNCHING OR GRABBING: METHOD A

1. As the opponent tries to punch you or grab you while you are lying on the ground, block the opponent's arm with your left foot.

2. Place your left foot to the side of the opponent's knee of his front leg.

3. By hooking your right foot behind the opponent's front foot and pushing it from inside with your left foot, throw him backward. Escape immediately or, if it is absolutely necessary, attack the opponent to subdue him.

Practice variations of this technique, such as the opponent coming from your left side.

PUNCHING OR GRABBING: METHOD B

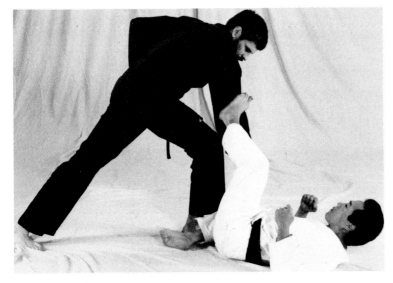

1. As the opponent tries to attack you with a punching or grabbing motion while you are lying on the ground, block his attacking arm with your left foot.

2. Bring your left foot to the outside of the opponent's front leg, and bring your right foot behind it.

3. By the scissor motion of your left foot pulling and your right foot pushing the opponent's front leg, throw the opponent to his right side.

Practice variations of this technique, such as the opponent coming from your left side.

CHOKING: METHOD A

1. While you are lying on the ground, the opponent tries to choke you. (In this case, assume the opponent is on your right side.)

2. Bring your right knee against the opponent's stomach by tucking it in tightly.

3. Push the opponent away with your right leg. Also use the strength of your left leg by pushing your left foot on the ground.

4. Break the opponent's hold as you straighten your left leg.

5. Kick the opponent's chin with your left foot and escape.

Practice this from the other side as well. (Assume the opponent is coming from the left side.)

CHOKING: METHOD B

1. As the opponent tries to grab your neck while you are lying on the ground, catch his hand before it reaches you.

2. Immediately begin to twist the opponent's hand with both your hands. Twist it in such a way that the palm side faces him.

3. Both your thumbs meet at the back of the opponent's hand. Push the ground with both feet, and feel the power in your stomach.

4. Throw the opponent to his right as you continue to press on his right wrist.

5. Keep holding his hand as he falls on his side.

6. You may finish the technique by delivering a kick to the opponent's face. Or you may just get up and escape, if it's possible.

Suppose you catch the opponent's left hand or the opponent comes from your left side. Try different possibilities.

CHOKING: METHOD C

1. While you are lying on the ground, the opponent has actually reached your neck with both his hands.

2. Kick the opponent's face with your left foot, or you may be able to kick the side of his body with your left knee.

3. As he temporarily becomes a little weak from your kick, grab his hand with both your hands.

4. Once you have succeeded in grabbing his hand, start to press his wrist.

5. Raise your upper body as you throw the opponent on his back by continuing to press on his wrist.

CHOKING: METHOD D

1. While you are lying on the ground, the opponent has actually reached your neck with his hands.

2. Tuck your right knee in against the opponent's stomach, and stretch it to kick his chin with your right foot.

3. After kicking the opponent's chin, use your right leg to break his hold.

4. Escape as soon as you can by rolling away from the opponent.

Practice this technique from the other side as well. (Assume the opponent is coming from your left side.)

4 Falling Techniques

The falling method, commonly referred to as *ukemi*, is extremely important in the practice of any martial art.

The most important aspect of the falling method is protecting the head when you land. To do so, tuck your chin tightly as though you were making your whole body into a small ball.

Your arm(s) should bear the weight of your fall the moment you hit the ground. In side falling, receive the whole impact of falling with either arm. In front or back falling, naturally use the two arms, as shown in the following illustrations.

SIDE FALL

1. Bring your right arm above your left shoulder with its palm showing away from your face.

2. As you take the fall sideways, make sure that your weight is sustained by your right arm. The falling arm (the right arm, in this case) is straight, and it is at about a 45-degree angle from the body.

SIDE FALL FROM THE STANDING POSITION

1. From a natural stance (see page 55), bring your right foot in front of your left foot. At the same time, bring your right arm across your chest in front of the left shoulder. The palm faces downward, and your eyes are directed to where you are about to fall.

2. Bend your knees and lie down sideways, simultaneously taking the fall with your right arm. Your weight should be placed on the falling arm (the right arm) as much as possible.

3. As you practice regularly, it becomes easier to fall with more speed and power.

4. The most important falling technique is to protect the head by tucking the chin in. The falling arm is straight, and it should be about 45 degrees from your body. Relax your legs by bending the knees a little. Do not cross your legs.

BACK FALL

1. From the sitting position, cross your arms in front of your chest with the palms facing down.

2. As you fall backward, raise your arms high above your forehead.

3. As you land, slap both hands hard on the floor. The arms are straight and about 45 degrees from the body.

4. Do not hit your head on the floor. To avoid this, keep your chin tucked in tightly. Relax your legs by bending the knees.

FRONT FALL

2. As you land, protect your face by slapping the floor with both forearms. Support your body with your forearms and the balls of your feet.

1. Start in the kneeling position with your hands in front of your face with palms facing forward.

3. As you get used to this falling technique, you may also try it from the standing position.

4. Your face should be turned either to the left or to the right at the moment you land.

FRONT ROLLING FALL

1. Take one step forward with your right foot.

3. Roll along the line of your right arm to your right shoulder. (Do *not* touch your head as you roll.)

2. Bend over and place your left hand on the floor in a straight line from the right foot. Then place your right knife hand between the right foot and the left hand.

4. As you finish the rolling motion, come up with the left arm falling. This is the same finishing form as the side fall from the sitting position.

Try the other side as well. (Start with the left foot forward, and take the final fall with the right arm.)

5 The Practical Karate

Karate began as a form of physical exercise and self-defense. This martial art is now also highly regarded as a competitive sport and as a means of building character.

In all its fullness, traditional karate includes many levels of intricate, subtle, and profound techniques. Mastering them requires not only self-discipline and patience, but also instruction by a good teacher.

Practical karate, however, refers only to the basic form of the art-sport that helps one to become physically fit and to defend oneself. Practical karate focuses on the application of techniques to real self-defense situations and uses techniques that are relatively easy to learn on one's own. (A book, however, can never replace good instruction by a teacher.) All techniques presented in this book are, once mastered, applicable to self-defense situations.

Although not as intricate as traditional karate, practical karate provides all the necessary ingredients—mental and physical—to make one more proficient in self-defense.

BASIC STANCES

To deliver a strong and effective technique, you must develop a strong, stable stance. Through trial and error, karate masters in earlier times developed different stances for different techniques. These stances are the foundations of techniques. Like a beautiful building, which is nothing if its foundation is weak, a fancy move or beautiful technique is useless if executed from a weak and unstable stance.

Comparing the foundations of buildings and stances must end here, however, because they are different on one very important point: dynamics. Stances in karate must be dynamic, allowing you to make a smooth and stable transition from one stance to another. You must be able to maintain the balance of the whole body during and after the execution of techniques, whether defensive or offensive. It may be effective to practice the various stances described in this book in combination and in sequences. Sequences include moving from the natural stance to the front stance, from the straddle stance to the back stance, and so on. Practice in stances increases your awareness of your center of gravity and helps to increase your balance as a whole.

Transitional movements include forward movement, which uses the method *yori-ashi*. In yori-ashi, go forward toward the opponent by pushing your rear foot to the ground while simultaneously moving your front foot forward. You then immediately move your rear foot forward.

Another transitional movement is *hiki-ashi*, which is used in backward movement. In hiki-ashi, you retreat by pushing your front foot to the ground while simultaneously moving your back foot backward. You then immediately move your front foot backward.

In either movement, the most important element is balance, which you maintain by keeping your center of gravity constant. In other words, you should not let your head bounce up and down too much, but maintain it at the same level at all times.

BASIC STANCES

ATTENTION STANCE: METHOD A

Open your feet approximately 45 degrees in each direction. Place your heels together.

ATTENTION STANCE: METHOD B

Place your feet together in parallel. In attention, you must still keep the shoulders relaxed and maintain quiet power in the lower abdomen.

NATURAL STANCE

Open your feet about the length of one shoulder width, with your feet pointing 45 degrees outward. Stand with the shoulders relaxed, and do not tense your knees.

PARALLEL STANCE

Place your feet in parallel at a distance of one shoulder width. Relax your knees and shoulders.

INVERTED NATURAL STANCE

From the parallel stance, turn your feet inward to about 45 degrees. Keep your back straight, and bend your knees inward slightly.

HOURGLASS STANCE (*SANCHIN DACHI*)

This is also referred to as the "tension stance" by some people. Open your feet to one shoulder width. Bend both knees with inward tension, as if you were protecting the groin area. The front foot points 45 degrees inward, while the back foot points straight forward. (The outside line of the foot is straight.) Drop the hip slightly with power in tan-den.

FRONT STANCE

To form the natural front stance, place your feet apart at shoulder width and take two natural steps. The front foot points straight forward, while the back foot points about 45 degrees outward. (The outside line of the front foot faces straight forward.)

The back knee is normally locked, while the front knee is bent in such a way that it rests directly above the tip of the toes. About 60 percent of the weight is placed on the front leg. Keep your back straight with a feeling of pushing your stomach outward.

NARROW FRONT STANCE

Open your feet to one-half of the shoulder width.

STRAIGHT FRONT STANCE

Align your feet with the front foot pointing straight ahead while the back foot points directly sideways.

STRADDLE STANCE

Open your feet as much as two shoulder widths. Point your feet straight forward, and bend your knees with their tension outward. Keep your back straight with the shoulders relaxed. Place your feet on the floor with the feeling of the toes tightly grasping the surface of the floor.

STAMPING STANCE

Some refer to this stance as "sumo wrestler's stance," and it is formed from the straddle stance by turning both feet out about 45 degrees. Keep your back straight with the feeling of pushing your stomach out.

HALF-AND-HALF STANCE

Distribute your weight evenly on both legs with the feet pointing in the same direction. Bend your knees equally for balance and stability. This is a strong defensive stance.

CAT STANCE

Support most of your weight on the back leg, and place your front foot on its ball to balance and direct your posture. Point your back foot about 45 degrees outward.

The knee of your front leg should be turned slightly inward with the feeling of protecting the groin.

BACK STANCE

Support about 70 percent of your weight by your back leg. Align your heels. Feel the power on the ball of the front foot. Bend your front knee slightly for flexibility.

MINOR BACK STANCE

Open your feet to one-half of the back stance. Distribute your weight in the same way as in the back stance.

MODIFIED BACK STANCE

Your feet are aligned and your weight distributed in almost the same way as in the regular back stance. Pull your upper body away from the opponent at the moment of blocking.

HOOK STANCE

Most of your weight is placed on the front leg. Bring the other foot behind the front leg in such a way that the shin of the back leg presses the calf of the supporting leg. This is primarily a transitional stance and lacks stability.

EXTREME CAT STANCE

From the regular cat stance, lower your body by bending your knees. This stance is the form to catch the opponent's kicking foot before its execution.

CRANE STANCE

METHOD A

Stand firmly with your weight on one leg. Place the other foot in front of the knee of the supporting leg.

METHOD B

Stand firmly with your weight on one leg. Place the other foot behind the knee of the supporting leg.

In both crane stances, balance is crucial. Your supporting leg should be strong and its knee slightly bent for stability.

HALF-TURNED BODY STANCE

Distribute your weight evenly on both legs. Point the front foot forward and the back foot sideways.

NATURAL STANCE

The natural stance appears to be the easiest of all karate stances. It is, indeed, the most basic one, the importance of which is often overlooked. As you study the art-sport of karate with care, you will learn the vital aspects of this stance.

Importantly, the shoulders must be relaxed, and you must feel power in the lower abdomen, or *tan-den* (colloquially *hava*), which is 1½–2 inches below the navel. Throughout the history of the martial arts, tan-den has been regarded as the source of human strength and the psyche. As you assume the natural stance, you should keep your head upright and direct your eyes forward. Your chin should be pulled in slightly in a natural way. Your breathing should be quiet and even, and air should be inhaled and exhaled through your nose. You should feel the power in your legs but not tense them too much.

The natural stance is the preparatory form as well as the finishing one. It is also referred to as "mercury's standing method." Mercury is easily and quickly diffused, but when the droplets gather together again, they quickly reconstitute themselves as a whole. Similarly, your initial natural stance should be ready to move in any direction at any time—yet be restored to its original position as quickly and smoothly as it can spread.

Movement to and from the natural stance is in harmony with your will and in accordance with the needs of the situation you confront. Seemingly the simplest stance, the natural stance, includes one of the most profound fighting principles in the martial arts.

BASIC FISTS

Basic fists, illustrated as follows, are necessary for both offensive and defensive techniques in karate.

In making these fists, be sure to keep the little finger as tightly bent in as the other fingers; this helps the whole fist become tighter. Also, to avoid injury to your wrist, keep the back of the wrist straight in relation to the target—and make contact mainly with the back of the first two knuckles.

BASIC FISTS: METHOD A

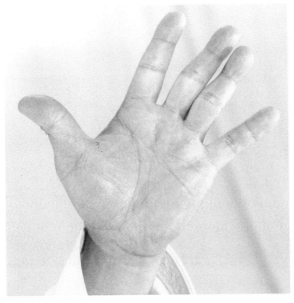

1. Open your hand fully.

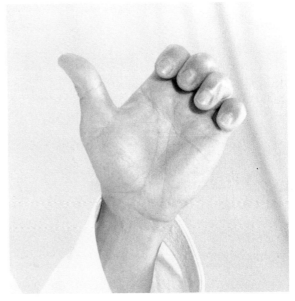

2. Bend the four fingers to touch their tips on the top of the palm.

3. Bend them once again fully and tightly. Make sure that the little finger does not become loose.

4. Press the index finger with the thumb.

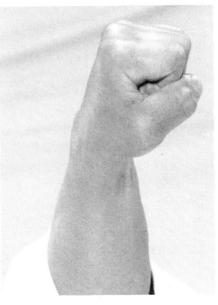

5. Keep the back of your wrist straight. The first two knuckles are the point of contact with the target.

BASIC FISTS: METHOD B

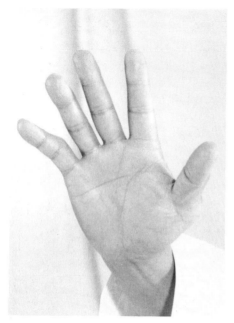

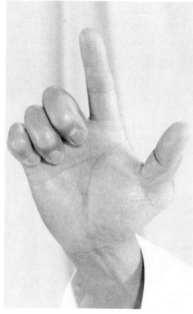

1. Open your hand fully.

2. Bend three fingers, leaving the index finger extended.

3. Bend the three fingers once again to touch their tips on the top of your palm. Make sure that the little finger is bent tightly.

4. Bend the index finger once to touch its tip on the bottom of your palm.

5. This is essentially the same fist as the first method.

6. Keep the back of the wrist straight. The point of contact with the target consists mainly of the first two knuckles.

PUNCHING

Karate punching involves several important points:

- The punching hand travels the shortest distance to the target. The hand travels in a straight line between the starting point and the target, so it is important to rub the elbow of the punching arm against the side of the body.
- Keep the shoulders relaxed at all times, feeling power in the lower abdomen and utilizing the muscles of the stomach and under the armpit. At the moment punching is executed, all the muscles should be tensed, including those in the chest and back.
- Try to synchronize the pulling arm and punching arm, emphasizing the action-reaction principle.
- Speed is important in karate technique. The simple but important principle applied in karate is mass times velocity squared equals *power* ($m \times v^2 = p$). The principle implies that power can transcend the size of the practitioner through the application of correct techniques.

PUNCHING: METHOD A

1. Place your punching hand (the right) just above the hipbone with its palm side up. Extend your pulling arm (the left) straight in front.

2. The pulling hand (the left) is important in karate punching, because the basic principle of action-reaction must be applied in executing punches. Do not twist the punching fist too early. Wait until the elbow passes the body.

3. Push the punching hand out straight, with its elbow rubbing the side of the body, thus making sure that the fist travels the shortest route to the target by following a straight line.

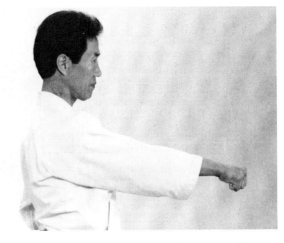

4. Relax your shoulders at all times. Try to synchronize the two arms—punching and pulling.

PUNCHING: METHOD B

1. Repeat the punching motion with both arms slowly many times until you feel comfortable with it.

2. Ultimately, the punching power comes from the lower abdomen (tan-den) as well as the muscles below the armpit.

3. The *lunge punch* is executed by the hand on the same side as the front leg.

4. The *reverse punch* is executed by the hand opposite the front leg.

PUNCHING: METHOD C

◁1. Let's look at the punching method from a different angle. From the natural stance, extend the pulling hand straight in front of you.

2. The punching arm (the right) must brush the side of your body as it moves forward. ▷

◁3. Do not twist the fist of the punching arm until its elbow passes the side of your body.

4. At the moment you execute the punch, your fist is fully twisted. Normally the first two knuckles of the fist are the main points of contact with the target. ▷

◁5. Reverse the process to practice with the other arm.

6. Make sure that your shoulders are relaxed at all times, while you feel power emanating from the lower abdomen at the moment of punching. The muscles below the armpits also play an important role in delivering a powerful punch. ▷

HANDS AND ARMS AS WEAPONS

Human hands and elbows are natural weapons for offense and defense. The first "attack" made by one human being on another was probably done with hands. Even today, one popular sport is boxing, which brings offensive and defensive uses of the hands to a high level.

Hand technique in karate is, of course, different from that used in boxing. A karate practitioner wishes to stop the opponent with one punch, while a boxer throws as many punches as possible until his opponent goes down. Boxing, of course, is a sport that uses gloved hands, while karate uses bare knuckles, in self-defense.

One-knuckle fists (see page 92) are particularly effective in self-defense because they can overpower the opponent with relatively little force.

When karate punches are executed, the hips, legs, and trunk must move simultaneously to complete the technique effectively. Speed is also important in producing an effective punch, as reflected in the basic principle $m \times v^2 = P$. (In other words, it is possible for a small person to produce a greater power than a larger person by applying more velocity as he executes the technique.) The true source of power as in any other karate technique, is tah-den (lower stomach).

STRAIGHT PUNCH

1. The straight punch can be delivered at the opponent's solar plexus.

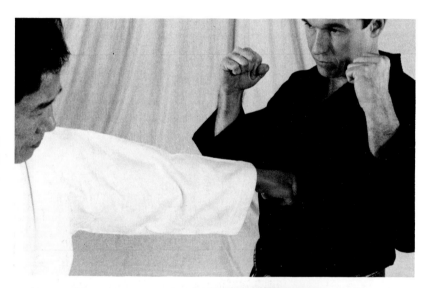

2. The straight punch can be delivered at the opponent's temple.

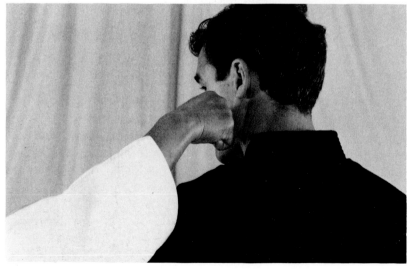

3. The straight punch can be delivered at any part of the face, especially at the philtrum.

4. Any part of the midsection, the abdominal area in general, can be a target.

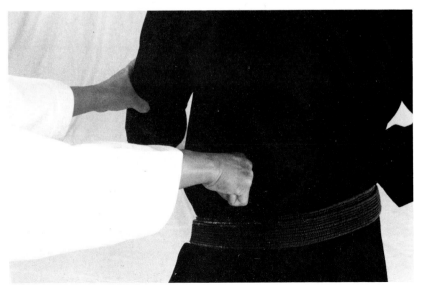

5. The kidney also can be an effective target for the straight punch.

LUNGE PUNCH

1. Block the opponent's front kick with your left arm.

2. Lunge forward and execute the right punch to the opponent's midsection or face. Execute the punch with the hand on the same side as the front leg.

REVERSE PUNCH

1. Block the opponent's left upper punch with your left arm.

2. Grab the attacking arm and deliver the right reverse punch to the opponent's face. Execute the punch with the hand on the side opposite the front leg.

KNIFE-HAND STRIKE

Basic Knife-Hand Strike

1. Bring your striking hand high above your shoulder and behind the head with the palm facing out.

2. Twist the striking hand in such a way that the palm of the knife hand faces upward. Retract the pulling arm in a synchronized manner.

3. At the moment you strike the target, make sure that the knife hand is tightly formed. Use the snapping motion of your striking arm's wrist and elbow. Relax your shoulders as you execute the technique.

4. As you block the upper attack, prepare immediately for the knife-hand strike.

5. The target can be the temple, neck, or even ribs (by the horizontal knife hand).

6. In the case of an inside-outward knife-hand strike, the striking hand is placed above the shoulder of the other side with its palm side facing upward.

7. A proper stance and the hip rotation are very important in an effective knife-hand strike. It is often used with a wide stance.

Inside-Outward Knife-Hand Strike

1. Face the opponent in the ready-to-defend position.

2. Block the opponent's left upper punch with your left arm.

3. Grab the attacking arm and prepare for the knife-hand strike from inside outward.

4. Execute the inside-outward knife-hand strike horizontally to the opponent's throat. It also can be delivered against the opponent's solar plexus in the same manner.

Outside-Inward Knife-Hand Strike

1. Face the opponent in the ready-to-defend position.

2. Block the opponent's left upper attack with your left arm.

3. Immediately grab the opponent's attacking arm with your left hand, and pull him forward to take him off balance.

4. Execute the knife-hand strike to the opponent's temple.

5. An effective alternative is to execute the horizontal knife-hand strike to the opponent's solar plexus.

BACK-FIST STRIKES

Sideways Back-Fist Strike

1. Fully bend the elbow of your striking arm.

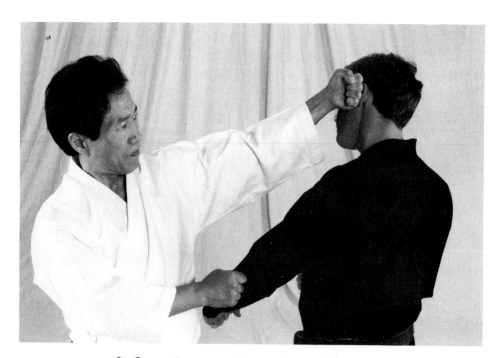

2. Snap the arm sideways at the elbow, and strike at the opponent's temple with the sideways back fist.

Reverse Sideways Back-Fist Strike

1. Begin with the fist of the striking arm positioned with the palm side up.

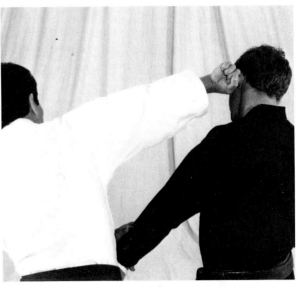

2. As you twist the fist so that the palm side turns away from the target, strike at the temple.

Downward Back-Fist Strike

1. Begin with the fist turned so that its palm side faces the opponent.

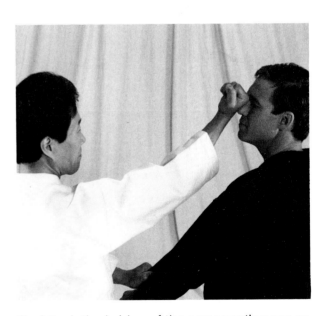

2. Attack the bridge of the opponent's nose or his philtrum with the back-fist strike as you twist your fist at the moment of striking.

RIDGE-HAND STRIKE: METHOD A

1. Extend your pulling arm straight in front of you.

2. Move your striking hand from the side of your hip with a slight circular motion.

3. Synchronize the striking arm and the pulling arm.

4. Block the opponent's left upper attack with your left arm.

5. Grab and pull the attacking arm to put the opponent off balance.

6. Execute the right ridge-hand strike to the opponent's left temple.

RIDGE-HAND STRIKE: METHOD B

1. Face the opponent in the ready-to-defend position.

2. Block the opponent's left upper attack with your left arm.

3. Grab the opponent's attacking arm, and pull him forward to put him off balance.

4. Execute the ridge-hand strike to the opponent's temple.

5. This strike can also be delivered to the opponent's midsection.

ELBOW STRIKES

Upper-Elbow Strike

1. After blocking the upper attack, grab the opponent's attacking arm, and prepare for the upper-elbow strike with the other arm.

2. Before striking, the fist of the striking arm has its palm side up. At the moment you deliver the upper-elbow strike, the palm side is toward your face.

Back-Elbow Strike

1. By dodging the upper attack, spin and get ready for the back-elbow strike. Extend your attacking arm with its fist facing so that the palm side is down.

2. In the preparing posture, the fist of the attacking arm has its palm side downward. At the moment you execute the back-elbow strike, the palm side faces up.

Downward-Elbow Strike

1. Stop the opponent's tackling motion by extending one of your arms. With the other arm, prepare the downward-elbow strike on the opponent's head or the base of his skull.

2. In preparation, the fist of the attacking arm has its palm side facing out; at the moment you execute the downward-elbow strike, it turns to face inside.

Front-Elbow Strike

1. Parry the attacking arm to either side, and prepare for the front-elbow strike. The fist of the attacking arm has its palm side facing in the same position as in punching.

2. Execute the front-elbow strike with the fist of the attacking arm positioned so that the palm faces down.

Side-Elbow Strike: Method A

1. After blocking or parrying the attack, prepare for the side-elbow strike. The fist of the attacking arm is positioned so that it faces up.

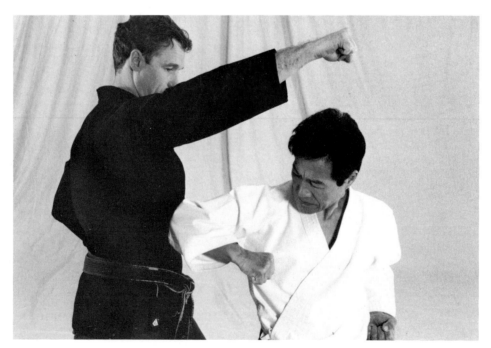

2. At the moment you execute the side-elbow strike, turn the attacking arm's fist so that the palm side faces down.

Side-Elbow Strike: Method B

1. Take the natural stance and prepare for the attack from your left side.

2. Block the upper attack from the left side with your left arm.

3. To prepare for the side-elbow strike, bring your left arm back and pull back the left foot slightly. Your left fist has its palm side upward at this moment.

4. Bring the left foot outside of the opponent's left foot, simultaneously executing the side-elbow strike with the left elbow. The palm side of the left fist turns down at the moment you execute the side-elbow strike.

HAMMERFIST STRIKES

Downward Hammerfist Strike

1. Bring your striking hand above your head with its palm side facing forward.

2. Bring the striking fist down as you twist it so that the fist shows its palm side inward at the moment of execution. Pull back the other arm at the same time as you strike down.

3. After the opponent loses his balance, you can strike the base of his skull with the hammerfist.

Horizontal Hammerfist Strike

1. Bring your striking fist to the side with its palm side facing out. Extend the pulling arm straight in front.

2. Twist the fist so that its palm side faces up as you strike.

Sideways Hammerfist Strike

The sideways (from outside inward) hammerfist strike is effective when executed against the opponent's solar plexus.

ONE-KNUCKLE FISTS

Index-Finger One-Knuckle Fist

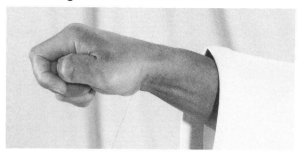

Press the inside of the index finger with the tip of the thumb as you push out the index finger's knuckle.

Middle-Finger One-Knuckle Fist

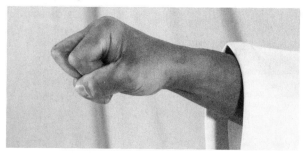

Push the knuckle of your middle finger out and press the finger's tip with the third finger and the index finger.

Applications

1. Block the opponent's right-lunge upper punch with the right arm.

2. Grab the opponent's attacking arm immediately with your blocking hand, and take the opponent off balance.

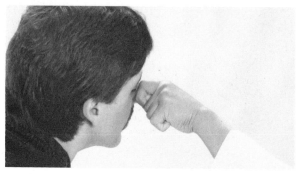

3. Attack the opponent with the index-finger one-knuckle fist to the eye.

4. The middle-finger one-knuckle fist to the ribs also can be an effective weapon.

SPEAR-HAND STRIKE

1. Block the opponent's left upper attack with your right arm.

2. By shifting your weight to the right leg, deliver the left spear-hand strike to the opponent's midsection.

3. The spear-hand strike can be used against the opponent's eye in the form of a two-finger spear hand.

4. It also can be executed against the opponent's throat.

BACK-FIST THRUST (NONTWISTED PUNCH)

1. Block the opponent's left upper attack with your left arm.

2. Grab the attacking arm and pull him forward to break his balance.

3. Execute the back-fist thrust to the opponent's ribs.

PALM-HEEL STRIKE

1. Block the opponent's right upper punch with your left arm.

2. Grab the attacking arm, and deliver the palm-heel strike to the opponent's chin. The palm-heel strike is executed in the same manner as the regular punch.

3. The palm-heel strike can also be executed against the opponent's jaw.

1. Block the opponent's left upper attack with your right arm.

2. Grab the attacking arm.

3. Execute the flat fist to the underside of the opponent's nose (philtrum). The flat fist can be executed in the same way as the normal fist.

HOOK PUNCH

1. Block the opponent's left upper attack with your left arm.

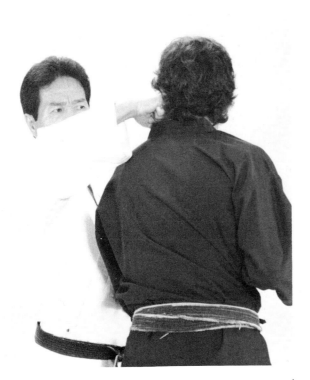

2. Grab the opponent's attacking arm, and execute the hook punch to his temple.

3. If the opponent delivers the right-hand punch, you can execute the hook punch to the opponent's solar plexus with your right hand from outside of his right arm.

DOWNWARD BLOCK–UPPER BLOCK THROW

1. Block the opponent's right front kick with the right-downward block.

2. The opponent immediately follows it with the right-upper punch, which you block with your left arm.

3. By grabbing the opponent's right leg and right arm, twist the opponent's body to your left and downward.

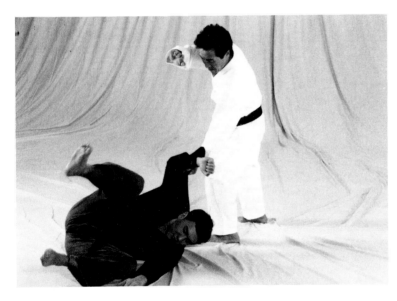

4. Keep holding the opponent's right arm as you complete the throw. You may finish the technique with a punch or a kick.

FEET AND LEGS AS WEAPONS

The main advantages of legs are, of course, their reach and size. With proper training, they are extremely effective weapons, particularly when you are fighting a large opponent. You can use legs and feet to offset your opponent's balance or just to create an opening for an effective hand technique to end a fight. Legs and feet are also effective finishing weapons themselves.

Balance is vital in any karate technique, but especially in foot and leg techniques. In the beginning stages of your training, you are bound to feel awkward and unstable as you try to stand on one leg while kicking with the other. The supporting foot should be placed flat on the ground at the moment you deliver the kick so that it can absorb the kick's impact without you losing your balance. For the maximum effect, it is important to push your hips and stomach toward the target at the moment you execute the technique.

FRONT KICKS

Basic Snapping Kick

1. Take the ready position.

2. Bring your kicking foot high with its knee fully bent.

3. Snap the knee and deliver the kicking foot to the target. Pull it back immediately.

Basic Thrust Kick

1. Take the ready position.

2. Bring your kicking foot high with its knee fully bent.

3. Thrust out the heel of the kicking foot with the hip pushing out toward the kick. It is important to pull back your kicking foot immediately after you have completed the motion.

**Snapping Kick and
Thrust Kick: Applications**

1. Assuming the opponent executes an upper-lunge punch, you execute the left-upper block.

2. Grab the attacking arm, and pull the opponent forward with both hands.

3. Execute the front-snap kick to the opponent's chin. Make sure that you snap your feet back immediately.

4. The low-front kick can be an effective technique to stop the opponent's attack or avoid it.

5. The front-thrust kick to the midsection with your heel can be effective.

6. To train yourself in the method of the thrusting kick, push the heel out to the target and the hip out with it in the same direction.

BASIC SIDE KICK FROM THE NATURAL STANCE

1. Take the ready position. Assume the natural stance and look toward the kicking target.

2. Bring the knee of your kicking leg high with its foot above the knee of the supporting leg.

3. Thrust your kicking foot directly through to the target. The kicking foot should show the edge of its foot to the target, with the toes curled up. Keep the supporting leg stable by bending its knee slightly. In the beginning, it is good to practice the low kick with the proper form.

4. In the middle kick, the kicking foot is directed to the opponent's ribs and midsection in general. The edge of the foot must be thrust out clearly with the toes curled up and the heel pushed out.

5. Do not drop your hands at the moment you execute the kick.

6. In the high-side kick, you may be able to kick the opponent's chin, neck, or even face. Balance is the important factor in any high kick.

BASIC SIDE KICKS: PRACTICE AND APPLICATION

1. Balance is extremely important in kicking techniques. In the side kick, the edge of the foot must be pushed out to the target, with the toes curled up and the heel pushed out.

2. In a self-defense situation, the low side kick can be an effective weapon to stop the opponent's aggression.

3. A high side kick to the opponent's chin or throat can be devastating, although it may not be practical in an actual self-defense situation.

4. The human body is usually more capable of moving forward than sideways. To be able to execute a side kick properly, you must stretch and exercise your body accordingly.

ROUNDHOUSE KICK FROM THE READY POSITION

1. Take the ready position.

2. Bring the kicking foot up by bending your knee.

3. Deliver the kicking foot to the target with a round motion. The supporting foot should be flat on the floor and stable. Bend the knee of the supporting leg slightly for balance and stability.

4. At the moment you kick, turn the supporting foot 90 degrees. Keep the upper body upright; do not bend unnecessarily.

5. Immediately after executing the technique, pull back the kicking foot.

6. By quickly pulling back the kicking foot, you can keep good balance after kicking.

ROUNDHOUSE KICK: APPLICATIONS

1. Block the opponent's lunge upper attack with the half-and-half stance.

2. Grab the attacking hand with your blocking hand. Immediately raise the knee of your leg high to prepare for the roundhouse kick. The knee of your kicking leg points to the target.

3. The low roundhouse kick is effective in self-defense situations.

4. To use the roundhouse kick to break the opponent's balance, deliver it against the back of the knee of the opponent's front leg.

5. The roundhouse kick to the opponent's midsection with the ball of your foot can be devastating.

6. The roundhouse kick can be used to attack the opponent's temple. Use your instep as well as the ball of the foot.

BACK KICKS

1. Begin with the natural stance.

2. Bring the kicking foot high by bending the knee, and look back over your shoulder at the target. Your supporting leg should be stable with its knee slightly bent.

3. Thrust your foot to the target so that the heel makes contact with the target.

4. At the moment you kick, the supporting foot should not move, and the toes should point down.

5. The back kick to the opponent's midsection, especially the solar plexus, can be very effective in a self-defense situation.

6. In a self-defense situation, the back kick to the opponent's groin area can be very effective.

7. You can break the opponent's balance and weaken his aggressive spirit by attacking his front knee with the back kick. In practice, it is good to start with the low kick with a good form.

8. You eventually may be able to kick the opponent's throat and chin with the high back kick.

9. Keep your eyes on the target as you execute the high back kick. Maintain good balance at the moment of kicking. Pull back the kicking foot quickly.

HOOK KICK

1. Assume the ready-to-kick position.

2. Bring the knee of your kicking leg high.

3. Bring your kicking leg to the target in an arc from the starting position. Move your hip away from the target at the moment you execute this kick.

4. The hook kick can be effective when applied to the opponent's temple with the ball of the foot.

5. Shown here is an example of the hook kick being applied to the opponent's temple area with the heel.

HOOK KICK: APPLICATION

1. Suppose you block the opponent's lunge punch with your left arm.

2. By adjusting the right foot slightly forward, prepare for the hook kick.

3. By continuous motion, throw the kicking foot to the target in an arc.

4. The hook kick with the heel to the opponent's midsection can be effective.

CRESCENT KICK

1. Assume the ready position.

2. In practice, extend the arm of the same side as the supporting leg.

3. Bring the knee of the kicking leg high before you execute the kick.

4. Bring the kicking foot toward the target in an arc. The hips should not be twisted much.

5. Bend the supporting leg slightly, and at the moment you execute the kick, it should not be moved much—at most 45 degrees on its ball.

CRESCENT KICK: APPLICATION

1. As you avoid the opponent's attack by stepping back, prepare for the countermotion.

2. Parry the opponent's attacking arm with the crescent kick.

3. When you are confronted by an opponent with a knife, arrange the distance carefully and try to find an opening.

4. As you find an opportunity, execute the crescent kick to parry the hand that holds the knife.

5. Block the opponent's attack.

6. Follow your block with a strong crescent kick to the opponent's midsection. This is an example of the crescent kick as an offensive weapon.

REVERSE ROUNDHOUSE KICK

1. Assume the ready position.

2. Bring the kicking foot (the left, in this case) high close to your right knee. The left knee is fully bent and points to the target.

3. Execute the reverse roundhouse kick by delivering the left foot from inside to outward. Maintain your balance by bending the supporting leg and pulling back the kicking foot quickly.

REVERSE ROUNDHOUSE KICK: APPLICATION

1. Execute the left-upper block against the opponent's right-lunge attack.

2. Grab the attacking arm, and bring the left foot high to prepare for the reverse roundhouse kick.

3. Keep holding on to the opponent's right arm as you execute the kick. Twist your body in such a way that the hip rotates toward the kicking foot.

BASIC BLOCKS

Blocking techniques were traditionally regarded as more important than attacking ones. Although not to be taken too literally, this view is consistent with the fact that the first movement of kata (see Chapter 7) consists of a block—a movement to be used only as a self-defense technique, never as an aggressive weapon.

Ideally, you should be able to defend yourself by blocking or dodging the attacks of your opponent(s) without resorting to counterattacks. For this reason, you must emphasize precision, power, and speed in blocking techniques.

UPPER BLOCK

1. From the natural stance, bring your right arm above your forehead with its hand open as shown.

2. Bring your left arm across your chest and under your right arm with the feeling of aiming at something above your shoulder with the left fist. Do not twist the left fist until the end of the procedure.

3. As you execute the left-upper block, your elbow should be bent about 120 degrees, and the forearm should be placed above the forehead with its palm side facing the opponent.

4. At the moment you execute the upper block, twist your fist in such a way that its palm side faces the opponent. The twisting motion gives power to the blocking arm. Do not try to scoop up the attacking arm; rather, try to deflect the attack with the correct method.

OUTSIDE-INWARD BLOCK

1. Bring your right arm to the ready-to-block position with the palm side of the hand facing down.

2. Without changing the face of the right fist, bring it to the midsection. Do not drop the elbow yet.

3. At the moment you block, twist your fist so that its palm side faces upward, and simultaneously drop down your elbow to complete the block.

4. Make sure that the elbow of the blocking arm does not leave the body too far.

INSIDE-OUTWARD BLOCK

1. Cross your arms in front of your chest with the blocking arm placed under the other. The fists both have their palm sides downward at this point.

2. Bring the blocking arm across the chest with its elbow as the center of movement. The pulling arm should slide on the inside of the elbow of the blocking arm as it is being brought back to the side of the hip.

3. At the moment you block, the palm sides of both fists face upward. The fist of the blocking arm should be placed at the shoulder level.

In executing this block, first make contact with the attacking arm as if you are scooping it from underneath; then push the arm sideward. Thus, your blocking arm is twisted in such a way that it ends up on top of the attacking arm.

DOWNWARD BLOCK

1. If your right arm is the blocking arm, bring the right fist to the left shoulder with its palm facing upward.

2. The blocking arm slides over the pulling arm. Keep the palm side of the blocking arm's fist facing upward.

3. At the moment you block, turn the fist of the blocking arm so that its palm side faces downward.

4. You can apply this blocking technique against a middle punch.

5. The most common application is against a kicking technique such as a front kick to your midsection or groin area.

KNIFE-HAND BLOCK

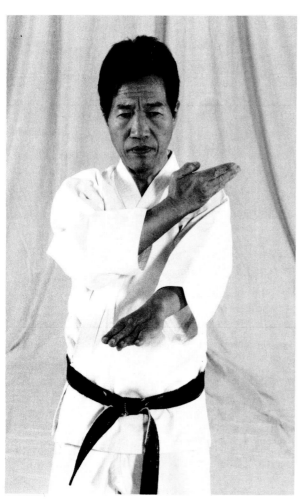

1. Bring the blocking arm (your right arm) to the other side of the shoulder with its palm facing up.

2. The right arm slides over the left arm with its palm still facing up.

3. At the moment you block, twist the hand of your blocking arm in such a way that the knife hand makes contact with the attacking arm.

4. This block is often used with the back stance.

SPECIAL BLOCKS

Blocks can be differentiated according to their purposes—such as getting away from or counterattacking the opponent. There are also blocks so devastating that you can "freeze" the opponent without any follow-up attack.

In an actual situation, use any block that comes to you naturally. Natural blocks are normally easy to execute if practiced well. Special blocks are presented here only for those who want more challenge in practices. You do not need to include them in your practice in the beginning. These special blocks are difficult to execute in an actual situation with effectiveness and speed. With constant practice, self-discipline, and patience, however, you may find those "special" blocks becoming more natural.

KNEE BLOCK

1. Assume the ready-to-defend position.

2. Bring the blocking knee high in the ready position.

3. Bring the knee in the roundhouse motion to the target.

4. This block can be used as a block against a punch.

5. It can be also used against a kick.

CRESCENT-KICK BLOCK

1. Assume the ready position.

2. Bring your kicking leg around in an arc to the target.

3. In practice, your other arm can be the imagined target.

4. As the opponent kicks, parry the opponent's kicking foot with the inner side of the sole as you perform the crescent kick.

CHICKEN-HEAD BLOCK

1. Make the knife hand with your blocking hand, and prepare for the block.

2. As you twist your hand so that its palm side faces inward, bring it up to block the attack.

3. Tense your wrist and bend it in order to hook the attacking arm with the side of the wrist to the first joint of the thumb.

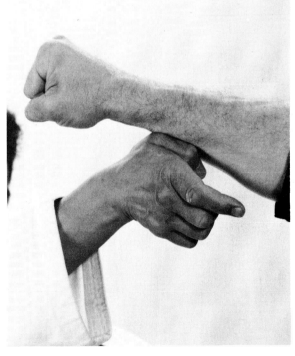

4. Snap your wrist and push the extension of the thumb to its first joint upward in order to block the attacking arm's forearm.

OPEN BACK-HAND BLOCK

1. Bring the blocking arm across your chest to the other side. Open the hand of the blocking arm and face its palm downward.

2. Do not twist your hand until it comes into contact with the target.

3. Deliver the block directly to the attacking arm's forearm, wrist, or elbow.

4. After the block, you can immediately grab the attacking arm and begin the counterattack.

BACK-WRIST BLOCK

1. Bring the blocking hand down. Open it and face its palm downward.

2. As you raise your wrist to block the attacking arm, push it up by putting the five fingers together so that it feels as though you are picking up something with them.

3. This block can be executed from the side as well to parry the attacking arm.

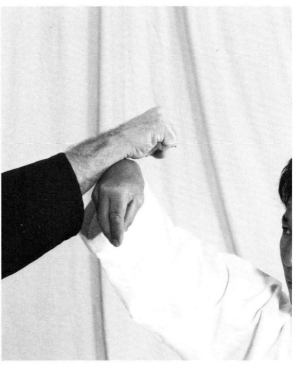

4. Make contact with the attacking arm at its elbow, forearm, or wrist.

PALM-HEEL BLOCK

1. Bring the blocking hand high above your shoulder with its palm facing down. Do not push the palm heel out yet.

2. As you are about to block the attacking arm or leg with the heel of your palm, bring your hand down as you push the palm heel out and down.

3. Press the heel of your palm against the attacking arm's forearm, elbow, or wrist. If you are blocking a kick, press the palm heel against the opponent's ankle or knee.

4. This block can be executed vertically as well as horizontally.

WEDGE BLOCK

1. Cross your arms in front of your chest with the palm side of your fists facing you.

2. Turn your fist as you make contact with the attacking arms, and bring your elbows closer to your body.

3. At the moment you block, the palm side of your fists should face the opponent. This block is effectively used with the back stance or the cat stance. Drop your hip down and back as your blocking arms make contact with the attacking arms.

4. You can use this block against an opponent who tries to choke you or grab your neck.

AUGMENTED BLOCK

1. Bring both arms to one side away from the attacking arm. Both fists have palm sides facing down in preparation.

2. Bring both arms toward the attacking arm as you twist the fists so that their palm sides face upward.

3. At the moment you block, place the blocking arm that makes contact with the attacking arm in the same position as in the inside-outward block. Press the blocking arm with the other hand in order to strengthen the effect of the block.

4. This block is usually executed with the back stance. In counterattack, one of the techniques may be a back-fist strike to the opponent's face by grabbing the attacking arm. (Needless to say, in counterattacking, one must shift the weight forward from the back stance.)

CROSS BLOCK

1. In preparation, place both hands at each side of your hips as in the ready position for punching.

2. In the upper-cross block, bring both arms straight, crossing at the wrists, to block the attacking arms above your forehead.

3. At the moment you block, press your crossed hands against each other at the wrists, pushing the attacking arm up.

4. This technique can also be executed with open hands.

5. Against the middle punch, apply the downward-cross block. Bring your crossed arms down from the sides of the hips. As you block the attacking arm, press the crossed hands down against the attacking arm.

6. The downward-cross block is often used against the front kick to the midsection. Make sure that your back is straight; don't lean forward when you block.

SCOOPING BLOCK

1. In preparation, bring the blocking arm above your shoulder with the palm side of the fist facing down.

2. Bring down the blocking arm, making an arc and twisting the hand so that its fist comes to face palm side up at the moment you block.

3. To make this block effective, twist your hip toward the blocking arm. This block can be executed from both directions: from inside outward and from outside inward.

4. In executing this block with outside-inward motion, if your blocking arm is the right arm, step back with the left foot at the moment you block. You can break the opponent's balance and counterattack by either throwing or punching.

TECHNIQUES AND PRESSURE POINTS AT A GLANCE

Proper execution of a technique by a physically fit practitioner is usually effective to a degree, no matter what part of the opponent's body is hit. However, many experts say that it is not how hard one hits or kicks, but what part of the opponent's body one attacks, that counts.

For maximum effect, practitioners should concentrate their blows on pressure points. Depending on the system used to count, there are about 72 points on the human body. Of course, one can't remember them all in an emergency, but you should be able to recall the most easily accessible: the face (philtrum); middle body (solar plexus); and lower body (groin). Other easily accessible points are the temples, the floating ribs, the knees, and the shin.

Knowledge of pressure points should belong only to those who won't abuse it or hurt others accidentally. This applies to both children and adults. Always use your knowledge responsibly.

2. Top of head by hammerfist strike.

1. Top of head by hammerfist strike.

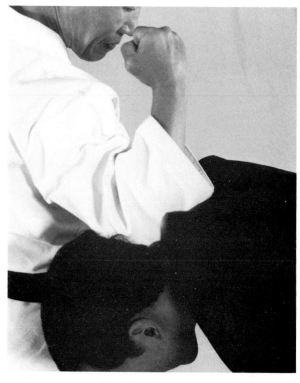

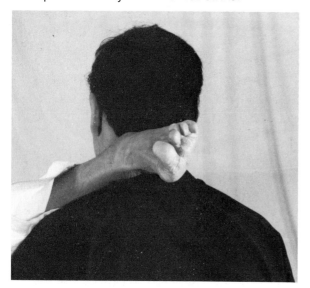

3. Base of skull by hook kick.

4. Base of skull by downward-elbow strike.

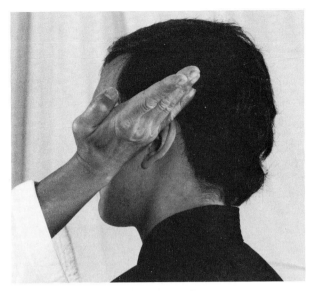

5. Temple by knife-hand strike.

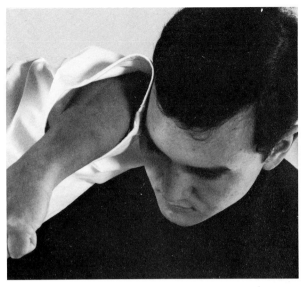

6. Temple by front-elbow strike.

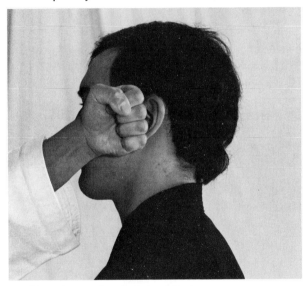

7. Temple by back-fist strike.

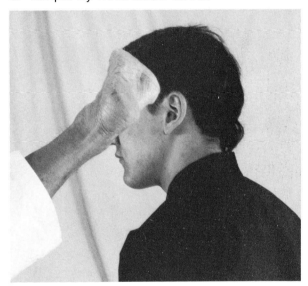

8. Head or temple by roundhouse kick.

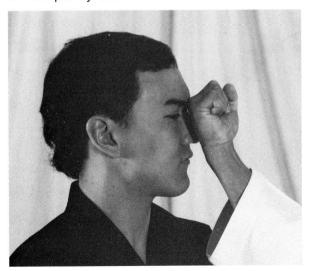

9. Bridge of nose by back-fist strike.

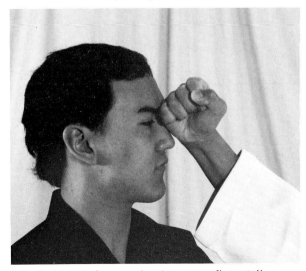

10. Bridge of nose by hammerfist strike.

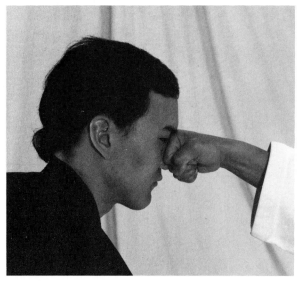

11. Bridge of nose by punch.

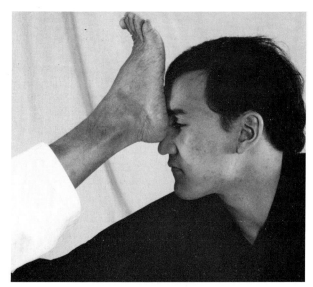

12. Bridge of nose by ax kick.

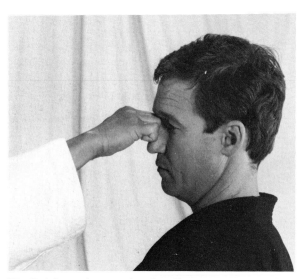

13. Bridge of nose by flat fist.

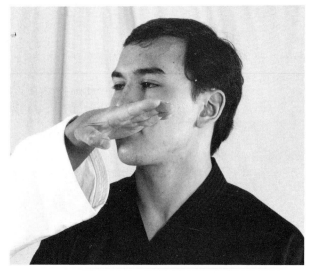

14. Philtrum by knife-hand strike.

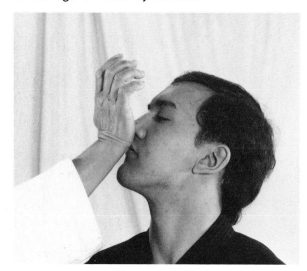

15. Philtrum by palm-heel strike.

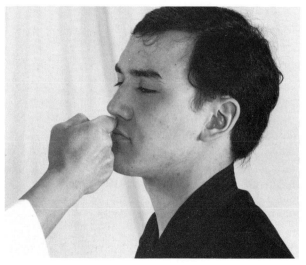

16. Philtrum by one-knuckle fist.

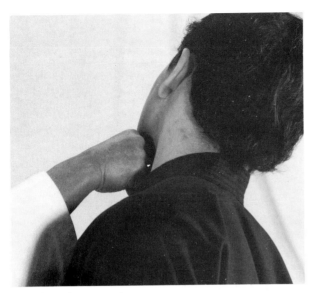

17. Jaw by punch.

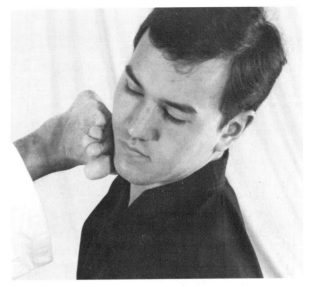

18. Jaw by roundhouse kick.

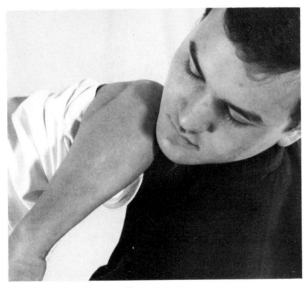

19. Jaw by front-elbow strike.

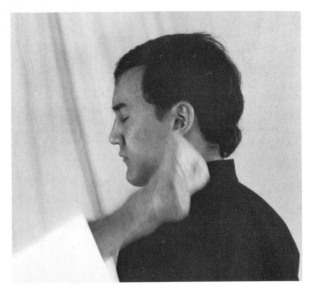

20. Jaw by roundhouse kick.

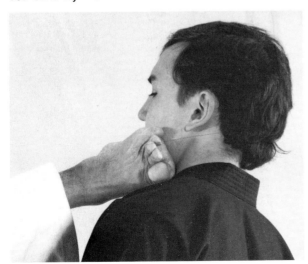

21. Chin by side kick.

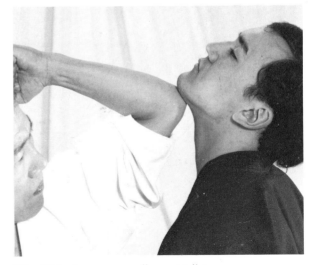

22. Chin by upper-elbow strike.

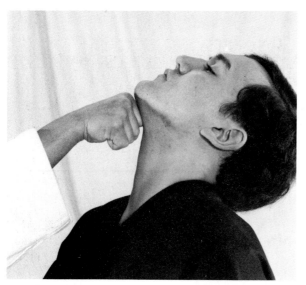

23. Chin by punch.

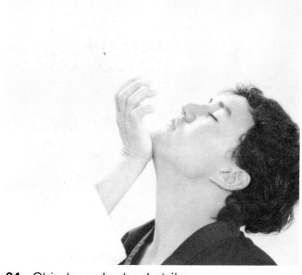

24. Chin by palm-heel strike.

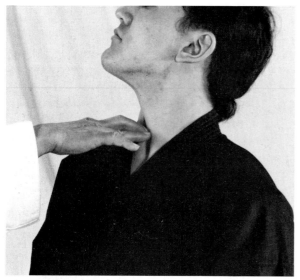

25. Adam's apple by spear hand.

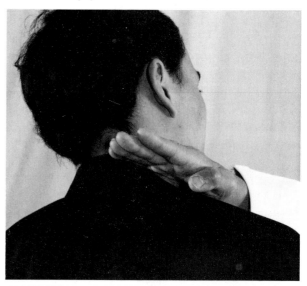

26. Side of neck by knife-hand strike.

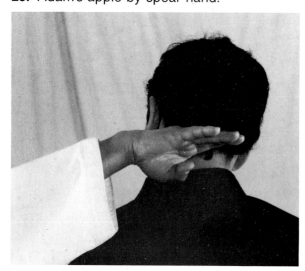

27. Back of neck by ridge hand.

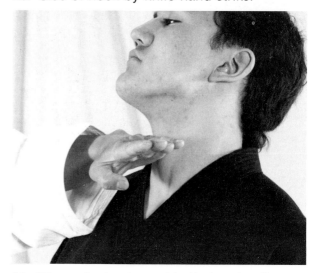

28. Throat by horizontal knife-hand strike.

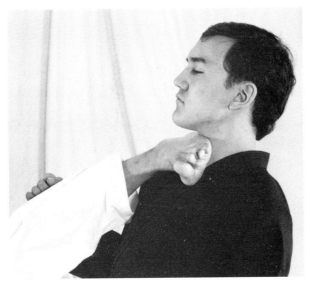

29. Throat by side kick.

30. Solar plexus by front-elbow strike.

31. Solar plexus by spear hand.

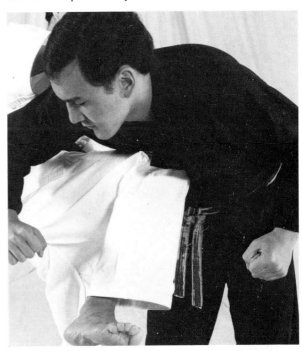

32. Solar plexus by roundhouse-knee kick.

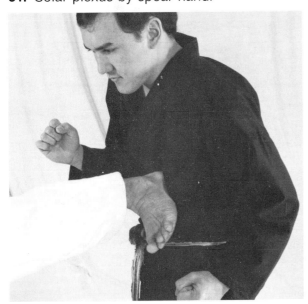

33. Solar plexus by back kick.

34. Solar plexus by side-elbow strike

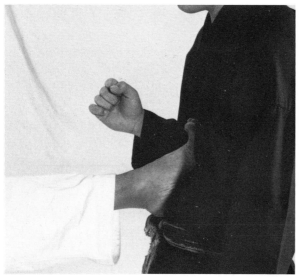

35. Solar plexus by front kick.

36. Solar plexus by front-elbow strike.

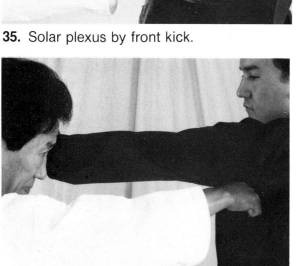

37. Armpit by punch.

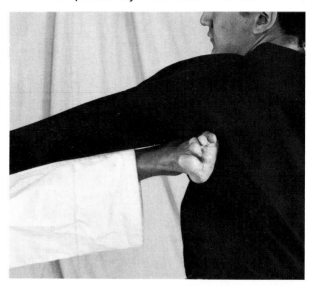

38. Armpit by side kick.

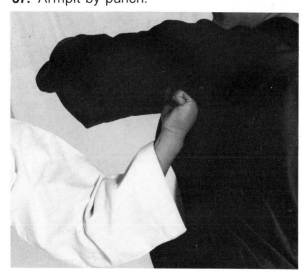

39. Armpit by back-fist thrust.

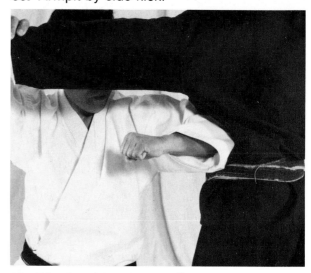

40. Ribs by side-elbow strike.

41. Ribs by side kick.

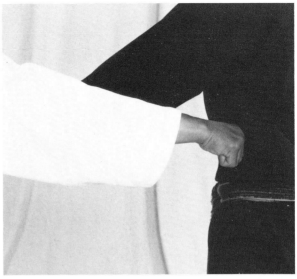

42. Ribs by punch.

43. Ribs by one-knuckle fist.

44. Ribs by punch.

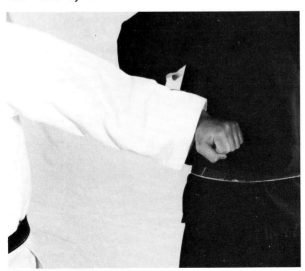

45. Kidney by hammerfist.

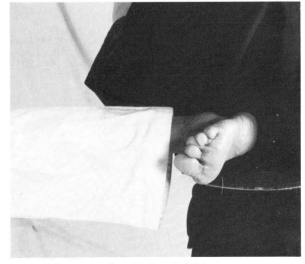

46. Kidney or ribs by hook kick.

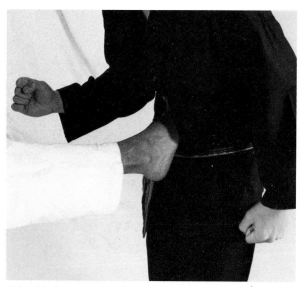
47. Abdomen by front kick.

48. Lower abdomen by front-knee kick.

49. Groin by back kick.

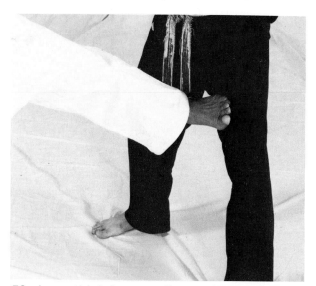
50. Inner thigh by roundhouse kick.

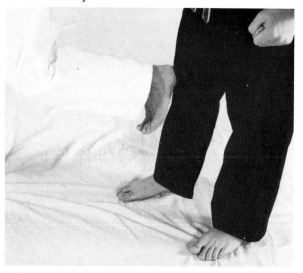
51. Front knee by back kick.

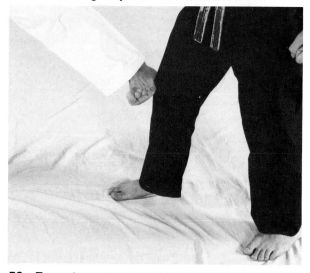
52. Front knee by side kick.

53. Inner knee by forearm strike.

54. Inner knee by knife-hand strike.

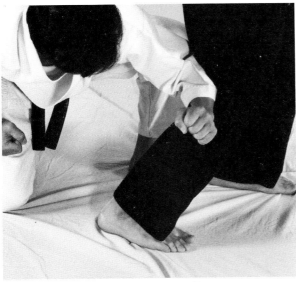

55. Back knee by forearm strike.

56. Back knee by side kick.

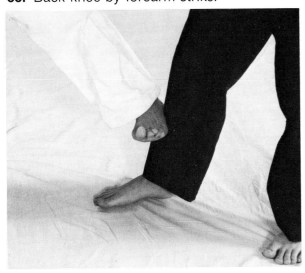

57. Shin by side kick.

58. Shin by back kick.

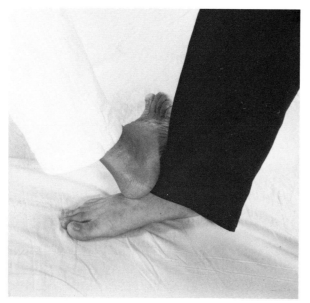 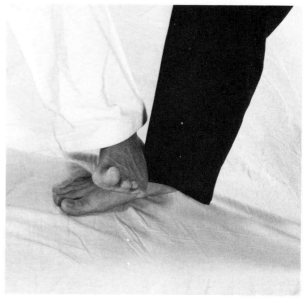

59. Instep by stamping with heel.

60. Instep by side-thrust kick.

THE RIGHT INTENTIONS

If you practice karate with the evil intention of hurting someone with your techniques, you will probably not make significant progress. Similarly, if you know that you are fighting for the wrong reasons, you may not be able to defend yourself well, either.

You must not harbor evil thoughts or ill will against others. In fact, ancient karate masters were strict in choosing their students, teaching only those of good character. The basic ethical principle of the art-sport of karate is based on the well-being of individuals and betterment of society as a whole.

Occasionally, you may hear that someone was hurt or even killed by an attacker who used karate techniques. But you must realize that anyone who would attack or hurt innocent people with a violent act is not a karate student. A true karate student never abuses or shows off his or her techniques. Karate training does not help people who engage in destructive behavior or antisocial conduct.

6 Advanced Self-Defense Techniques

The techniques presented in this chapter are considered "advanced" because their proper application requires not only physical expertise, but also a highly cultivated mind and spirit. Although real self-defense situations are not as neat and orderly as these exercises, intensive practice develops the qualities needed to apply these techniques at will—physical dexterity, a finely honed sense of timing and speed, inner confidence, and strong concentration. The techniques presented on the following pages are true "grammars" of self-defense that must be mastered to be used properly and effortlessly as the situation calls for them.

Please heed this special word about the exercises for self-defense against weapons. As repeated throughout this book, true self-defense situations are characterized by an infinite number of variables, such as the place of attack, your strength and speed relative to those of the opponent, and the opponent's mental condition. Situations in which weapons are involved may be even more complicated because of the many kinds of weapons available.

It is best and wisest, of course, to walk away or run away from any possibly dangerous situation. But especially against someone with a gun or a knife, you must use *extreme* caution in reacting to the situation. *In many such cases, the best method may be no resistance.* Your alertness and strength can help you determine whether you can possibly overcome your perpetrator and disarm him or her. Be careful, and if at all possible, don't resist.

Techniques described here are based on prearranged forms. Let me reiterate that real situations do not, naturally, present themselves in such a neat and systematic manner. Consider, therefore, these described techniques as grammars of self-defense that can help you develop many different techniques that apply in some situations. Cultivate your mental strength so that you can cope in any situation with calmness and confidence. And remember that in the real situations, you cannot expect the opponent(s) to act in a certain way. Take the following true story as a lesson.

A karate practitioner was provoked by a bully in the streets. Because he was experienced and proficient in the art of karate, the practitioner tried to ignore the bully and walk away. However, he was absolutely forced to defend himself. The bully had walked quickly toward him with a knife in his hand. Responding calmly and decisively, the karate practitioner realized he would be stabbed and seriously wounded. He thus walked into the bully and tried to grab the knife away from him. Although he cut his hand seriously, the karate practitioner kicked the bully in his groin and was able to prevent any further damage to himself.

ONE OPPONENT
HIP THROW

1. Dodge the opponent's upper attack to your right.

2. The opponent immediately tries to attack you with his left punch. Block it with the right-upper block.

3. Grab the opponent's left arm with your right hand, and pull him forward. Bring your left foot closer to the opponent's body.

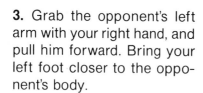

4. Again move your left foot closer to the opponent's left foot. At the same time, move your right foot inside the opponent's right foot. Place your left arm around the opponent's hip.

5. By using the strength of your hip and knees, lift and throw the opponent over your hip. Pull the opponent's left arm strongly.

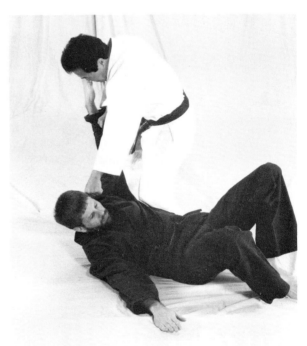

6. This should not require too much brute strength, for the opponent should go over your hip with a rolling motion in a flowing manner.

7. In practice, let your partner land on the floor gently, and make sure that he or she can take a good fall. In application, you may follow this with a punch or kick.

FROM UPPER BLOCK TO OUTER MAJOR SWEEP: METHOD A

1. Block the opponent's upper attack with your left arm.

2. Immediately grab the opponent's right hand with your left hand. Then step forward with your left foot next to the opponent's right foot. At this moment, push the opponent's left jaw with your open right hand.

3. As the opponent loses his balance a little, bring your right hand behind the opponent's back and execute the right roundhouse knee kick to the opponent's midsection.

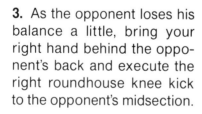

4. Bring your right leg behind the opponent's right leg to execute the outer major sweep. At the moment you throw, synchronize the three forces: push the jaw, sweep the leg, and pull the opponent's right arm.

5. As you throw the opponent, keep holding the opponent's right arm so that you can execute the finishing technique.

6. The finishing technique can be a punch or kick. Shown here is a kick to the opponent's face.

FROM UPPER BLOCK TO OUTER MAJOR SWEEP: METHOD B

1. Block the opponent's upper attack with your right arm.

2. Push down the opponent's attacking arm, and grab it with your left hand.

3. Attack the opponent's left jaw with the right palm-heel attack, simultaneously bringing your left foot next to the opponent's right foot.

4. Bring your right leg behind the opponent's right leg. Throw the opponent with the outer major sweep. Your calf makes contact with the opponent's calf for an effective throw.

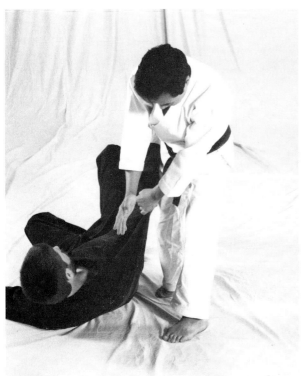

5. As you throw the opponent down, keep holding his right arm so that you have an opportunity for a finishing technique.

6. An example of a finishing technique is shown here with an attack to the opponent's temple with the left knee. The opponent's arm is locked over your right knee for submission.

FROM UPPER BLOCK TO ONE-ARM SHOULDER THROW

1. Block the opponent's upper attack with your left arm.

2. Grab the opponent's right arm and execute the upper punch (to make the opponent freeze for a moment).

3. Keep grabbing the opponent's right arm with your left hand as you bring your right foot inside the opponent's right foot. At this moment, bring your right arm under the opponent's armpit, and grab the opponent's shoulder with your right hand.

4. Pull your left foot all the way back to inside the opponent's left foot as you squat down securely. Do not bend your upper body forward too much.

5. With the strength of your hips and legs, lift the opponent up as you straighten your knees. Keep holding the opponent's choking arm, and pull it forward as you lift him. Your open left hand pushes up the opponent's left leg to help the throw.

6. Throw your opponent over your right shoulder in a flowing motion, not with a lifting-up motion. If you perform the technique correctly, it does not require brute force.

7. Keep holding the opponent's right arm as you complete the throw. In practice, this helps the partner to take a good fall. In a real situation, it helps you to follow up the throw with a kick or a punch.

8. A kick to the face can be effective in a real situation. In a street situation, you are throwing someone who has no knowledge of how to take a fall. Therefore, your opponent may lose much agressiveness at the time you throw him or her.

SHOULDER-WHEEL THROW

1. Block the opponent's upper attack with your right arm.

2. Grab the opponent's attacking arm and pull toward you, simultaneously executing the left back-fist thrust to the opponent's ribs.

3. Change the grabbing hand from the right to the left.

4. Get close to the opponent by sliding into him. Place your right shoulder underneath the opponent's stomach area. Your stance at this moment is a minor *shiko-dachi* (sumo wrestler's stance).

5. By using the strength or your hips and shoulders, lift the opponent high on your shoulders horizontally. You can more effectively use the springing motion of your knees if you don't open your feet too wide.

6. Throw the opponent down near the area in front of your left foot. Continue to hold the opponent's right arm with your left hand. (In practice, it is extremely important to use extra caution for the safety of your partner. Throw your partner in a gentle way so that he or she can take a good fall.)

7. Execute the finishing technique with a punch or kick, if necessary.

AGAINST A FULL-NELSON HOLD: CASE A

1. As you receive a full-nelson hold, kick the opponent's shin to freeze him.

2. Throwing a back kick to the opponent's groin can also weaken the opponent momentarily. Stepping on the opponent's instep can also be effective as a freezing technique.

3. Lean forward and grab the left side of the opponent's pants with your left hand.

4. Bring your left leg behind the opponent's right leg, while continuing to hold the left leg with your left hand.

5. Lift the opponent up and over your left thigh.

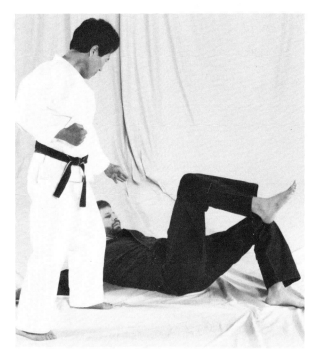

6. Shake the opponent off of your back.

7. Turn to the opponent on the floor and be ready to execute a finishing technique such as a punch or kick.

AGAINST A FULL-NELSON HOLD: CASE B

1. As you receive a full-nelson hold, stretch your arms high and bring your right foot outside the opponent's right foot.

2. Bring your left foot behind the opponent's right leg. With your right hand, hold the opponent's right arm and raise your left hand high to break the opponent's hold by his left arm.

3. Push the opponent back with your left arm and your whole upper body. The opponent's body falls over your left thigh.

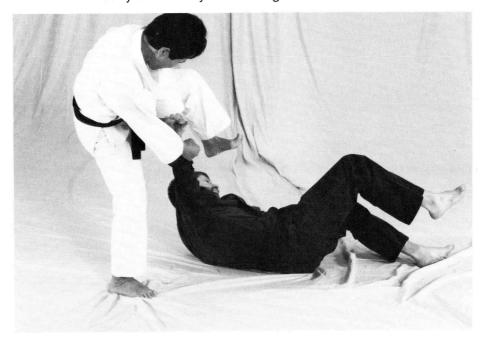

4. The finishing technique can be a kick or a punch. The important thing in this case is to keep holding the opponent's right arm after you have completed the throw.

TWO OPPONENTS

FROM THE SIDE-ELBOW STRIKE TO THE SIDE-ELBOW STRIKE

1. Block the attack of the opponent from the right side.

2. Slide in closer to the opponent and execute the side-elbow strike to the opponent's mid-section.

3. Place your right knee on the ground as you push the opponent's right knee from its inside with your right forearm. Grab the opponent's right foot with your left hand.

4. Forcefully push the opponent's right knee from inside with your right forearm as you pull the opponent's right foot strongly toward you.

5. As soon as you throw this opponent down, get on your feet and block the attack from the left side.

6. Follow the block with the side-elbow strike.

FROM SIDE-ELBOW STRIKE TO UPPER-ELBOW STRIKE

1. The opponent on your right side attacks you first. Block the attack with your right arm.

2. Slide in closer to the opponent, and execute the side-elbow strike to the opponent's midsection.

3. Block the upper attack by the opponent from your left side.

4. Grab the attacking arm, and execute the upper-elbow strike to the opponent's chin.

SIDE-ELBOW STRIKE AND FRONT-ELBOW STRIKE

1. You stand midway between two opponents.

2. The opponent on your left attacks you with an upper punch, which you block from the same stance.

3. Immediately counter-attack the opponent on the left with the side-elbow strike.

4. The opponent on your right attacks you with an upper punch, which you block from the straddle stance.

5. Grab the attacking arm, and pull it toward you to break the opponent's balance. Execute the front-elbow strike to the temple.

ROUNDHOUSE KICK TO THE HOOK KICK

1. Block the upper attack from your right side.

2. Grab the opponent's attacking arm, and execute the roundhouse kick to the opponent's face.

3. Immediately block the upper attack from the left side.

4. With your left heel, execute the hook kick to the opponent's left temple.

OPPONENTS IN THE FRONT AND BACK: CASE A

1. The opponent in front attempts to attack you, so dodge to your right side.

2. Bring your left foot in front of the opponent's left foot. By pulling back the right foot so that it is closer to the opponent's right foot prepare for the back-elbow strike.

3. Execute the back-elbow strike by pulling back the right elbow strongly.

4. You are now facing the opponent in the rear. Block the upper attack with your right arm.

5. Grab the attacking arm. By stepping in with your left foot closer to the opponent, execute the front-elbow strike to the temple.

OPPONENTS IN THE FRONT AND BACK: CASE B

1. Block the attack from the front with the upper-cross block.

2. Grab the attacking arm, and execute the up-and-down back-fist strike to the opponent's face with your right hand.

3. Turn to the rear and block the attack from that direction.

4. Immediately counterattack with the reverse punch to the opponent's midsection. You may keep the blocking arm where it is, or you may pull it back to the side.

OPPONENTS IN THE FRONT AND BACK: CASE C

1. Block the upper attack from the front.

2. Grab the attacking arm, and execute the strong front kick to the opponent's ribs.

3. With the same leg that you used to execute the front kick, deliver the strong back kick to the opponent in the rear.

OPPONENTS IN THE FRONT AND BACK: CASE D

1. You face one opponent in the front and are aware of another opponent in the rear.

2. Block the upper attack from the front.

3. Grab the attacking arm immediately and counterattack with the upper-elbow strike to the opponent's chin.

4. Turn to the opponent in the rear and block his upper attack.

5. Execute the side-elbow strike to the opponent's midsection by sliding toward him with both feet.

SIMULTANEOUS ATTACKS: CASE A

1. Block the simultaneous attacks from both sides. Your right arm executes the outside-inward block, and your left arm performs the inside-outward block.

2. Turn immediately to your left and grab the attacking arm. Execute the right back-fist thrust to the opponent's face.

3. As you hold on to the first opponent, counterattack the second opponent with the back kick.

4. Bring your left foot outside the first opponent's right foot and your right leg behind his right leg. You are now ready for the outer major sweep.

5. As you execute the outer major sweep, pay attention to the first opponent.

6. When you finish counterattacking both opponents, maintain awareness for "absolute domination" over the opponents.

SIMULTANEOUS ATTACKS: CASE B

1. Block the simultaneous attacks from both sides. Your right arm executes the inside-outward block, and your left arm executes the outside-inward block.

2. Immediately grab both attacking arms with your respective blocking arms. Pull down the right arm of the opponent on your right, and push away the right arm of the other opponent.

3. Counterattack the opponent on your right with the roundhouse kick to the groin or mid-section. Keep holding both arms.

4. As soon as you bring your right foot back to the ground after executing the roundhouse kick, attack the opponent on your left with a side kick to the midsection.

SIMULTANEOUS ATTACKS: CASE C

1. Simultaneous attacks from both sides come to your midsection. Block them downward with both open hands.

2. Hook the attacking arms with each of your respective blocking arms, catching behind the elbow of each attacking arm.

3. Immediately start to press the back of the elbow of each arm as you squat down and forward.

4. As you bring the opponents' heads closer to the ground, maintain intense pressure against the back of their arms.

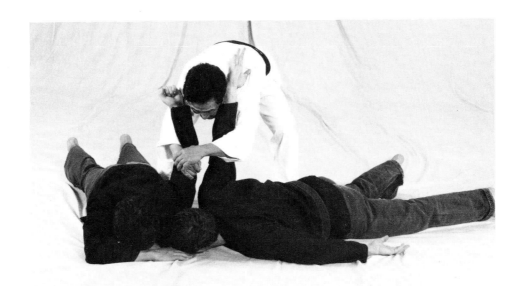

5. The submission is completed when the two opponents touch their heads to the ground and to each other. They are immobilized by the armlock. Squat down well, and don't be afraid to bend your knees if you find it necessary.

SIMULTANEOUS ATTACK: CASE D

1. You confront two opponents who stand at 45-degree angles on both sides (that is, one at NE and the other at NW).

2. The two opponents attack at the same time, and you block them with the double upper block. (It is true that this situation is highly unlikely, but these are grammars of self-defense, through which you learn various defensive techniques applicable to real situations.)

3. Grab both attacking hands. Push up the arm of the NW opponent, and pull down the arm of the NE opponent.

4. Keep controlling the left arms of both opponents by pushing up and pulling down the arms you hold. Step forward with the left foot.

5. Squat down and grab the NE opponent's right ankle with your right hand.

6. Scoop the NE opponent's right foot with your right hand and throw him down on his front.

7. Bring your right foot forward, and grab the NW opponent's right hand with both your hands.

8. As you pull your right foot closer to the left foot, go under the right arm of the NW opponent by grabbing his hand with both your hands. At this moment, turn to the south (the original rear).

9. You are now holding the opponent's right hand in such a way that both your thumbs meet at the palm of his right hand.

10. By pressing on the wrist of his right hand, throw down the NW opponent on his back as you take one step forward with your left foot. Make sure that you show zan-shin at the end of the techniques.

BOTH ARMS BEING GRABBED: CASE A

1. Both your arms are grabbed from both sides.

2. Free your left arm as you attack the opponent with the side kick.

3. Turn to your right and execute the left upper punch to the opponent on your right.

BOTH ARMS BEING GRABBED: CASE B

1. Execute a strong front kick to the opponent's midsection or groin, and free your left arm.

2. Turn to your right and do the same to the other opponent. (There are many possible counterattacks—combinations of kicks and punches.)

BOTH ARMS BEING GRABBED: CASE C

1. Both your arms are held from both sides.

2. Execute a strong side kick to the opponent on your left. The kick to the knee or the shin can be effective in a self-defense situation.

3. Free your left arm as you kick the opponent. Swing your left leg to the right, and use it to break the hold of the opponent on your right.

4. As you drop your left leg hard on the opponent's hands, break the hold.

5. Taking advantage of the opponent's being off-balance at this moment, execute a strong elbow strike to his head (the base of the skull).

BOTH ARMS BEING GRABBED: CASE D

1. Two opponents, one at each side, hold your arms.

2. Jump up with the feeling of going through a back flip and kick both opponents in their faces with the balls of your feet.

3. Show zan-shin—that you are alert and ready to respond to any further threat.

BOTH HANDS BEING GRABBED: CASE A

1. Both hands are being grabbed from two directions by two opponents.

2. Execute the strong hook kick to the opponent on your left. (Deliver the high hook kick to the opponent's temple.)

3. Adjust your left foot by crossing over the right foot, if necessary, and prepare for the next attack.

4. Execute the strong high hook kick to the other opponent's temple.

BOTH HANDS BEING GRABBED: CASE B

1. This is an excellent situation to practice the side kick.

2. Deliver the strong side-thrust kick against the opponent on your left. As you execute this kick to the opponent's midsection, pull your left hand from his hands.

3. Adjust your left foot by crossing over the right foot, if necessary, and prepare for the next attack.

4. With your right foot, deliver the strong side-thrust kick to the other opponent's midsection, and pull your right hand from his hands.

THREE OPPONENTS

CASE A

1. You are surrounded by three opponents: one in front and one at each side. With your right arm, block the attack from the front opponent.

2. Grab the attacking arm, pull the opponent forward, and execute the back-fist thrust to the opponent's midsection. The one-knuckle fist is effective in this case.

3. After executing the back-fist thrust, place your left forearm on the back of the first opponent's right elbow.

4. Press hard on the back of the opponent's right until he submits, and release it halfway to throw him on the ground.

5. Block the attack from the opponent on your left.

6. Grab the attacking arm, and execute the right-upper punch.

7. Place your right hand behind the opponent's right shoulder.

8. Execute the right roundhouse knee kick to the opponent's midsection.

9. Follow it with the outer major sweep. (Place your right leg behind the opponent's right leg immediately after the knee kick.)

10. Of course, punching and kicking often can be effective enough that you may not need any follow-up technique such as throwing. In practice, however, it is good to train yourself to follow through the counterattack to the end.

11. Block the attack from the opponent who was originally on your right.

12. Execute the strong side kick to the opponent's midsection.

13. Place your right foot behind the opponent's right foot after the side kick, and place your left arm across the opponent's shoulder. At the same time, place your right arm behind the opponent's right leg (the back knee).

14. By lifting the opponent's right leg and pushing his left shoulder, throw him backward. At the end of all these techniques, show awareness to the opponent in each direction.

CASE B

1. You are aware of being surrounded by three opponents; one in back and one at each side.

2. You are choked by the opponent in back. Press your chin down against the choking arm.

3. Grab the choking arm with your right hand and execute the strong back-elbow strike to the opponent's midsection.

4. Bring your left leg around behind the opponent's right leg. By pressing the back of the opponent's right leg with your left knee and pushing the upper body of the opponent backward with your left arm, throw him down on his back.

5. As you finish taking care of the first opponent, maintain the same concentration in dealing with the situation. Good balance is particularly important in a situation where you must deal with more than one opponent.

6. An upper attack comes from the opponent at the original left side. Block this attack with your left arm.

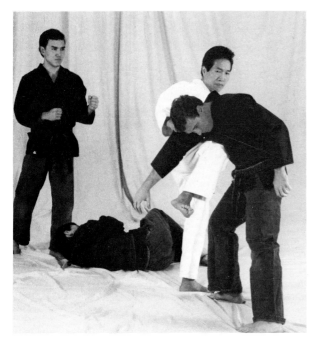

7. Grab the attacking arm, and execute the roundhouse knee kick to the opponent's mid-section.

8. The last opponent attacks you. Block this attack with your right arm.

CASE B (continued)

9. Grab the attacking arm with your left hand, and use your right hand to execute the backfist strike to the opponent's right temple.

10. After freezing the opponent with the backfist strike, squat on your right knee and place your right forearm against the inner knee of the opponent's right leg.

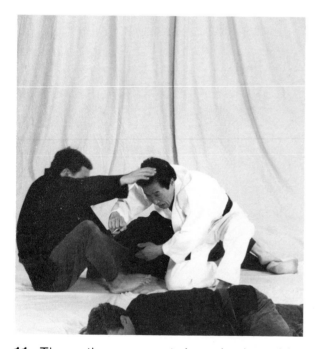

11. Throw the opponent down backward by pressing the inner knee of his right leg with your right forearm and by pulling his right foot with your left hand.

12. Demonstrate your mental attitude of awareness of the three opponents on the ground.

CASE C

1. You are aware you are surrounded by three opponents at your left, right, and rear.

2. As the opponent on your left attacks, execute the upper knife-hand block.

3. Deliver the strong knife-hand strike to the same opponent.

4. Execute the upper block against the attack from your original right.

5. Grab the attacking arm immediately, and execute the left-hand nontwisted punch to the opponent's ribs. You must slide a little toward the opponent to throw your hip into the technique.

6. As the opponent from your rear attacks, use your right arm to block with the right-upper block.

7. Spin counterclockwise, pivoting on your right foot and bringing your left foot back closer to the opponent. Execute the left back-elbow strike to the opponent's midsection.

8. At the end of the technique, show zan-shin—that you are alert and ready to respond to any further threat.

CASE D

1. Your opponents surround you from three directions—behind and on either side.

2. When the opponents on either side attack simultaneously, duck down on your right knee, and execute the double sideways punch with one-knuckle fists.

3. The opponent from behind attempts to grab your neck. Pull yourself away from this opponent and get on your hands and knees.

4. Execute the strong back thrust kick to the opponent's throat.

CASE E

1. The three opponents are in front and on both sides.

2. The opponent from your left side attacks you first. Execute the upper block with your left arm.

3. By grabbing the opponent's attacking arm with your right hand and pressing down the back of the opponent's right elbow with your left forearm, take the opponent down.

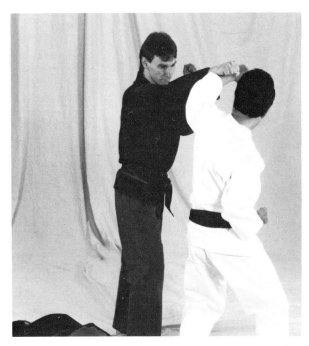

4. Execute the left upper block against the attack from the opponent in front.

5. Grab the attacking arm and execute the right upper punch.

6. After freezing the opponent by punching, grab his right hand in such a way that your two thumbs meet at the palm.

7. Go under the opponent's right arm by twisting your upper body and the opponent's wrist. Take him down backward by pressing on his wrist as shown.

8. The third opponent attacks you. Block this attack with your left arm.

9. Bring your left leg behind the opponent's right leg. Your left knee makes contact with the back of the opponent's right knee.

10. By pressing your left hand backward against the opponent's right shoulder, and by pushing your left knee against the back of the opponent's right knee, throw him backward.

11. In a real situation, you must be aware of the other opponents as you deal with one at a time.

12. The final attack can be a kick or a punch, depending on the situation. Of course, this is just a prearranged form of three-person attack. You must be able to apply these techniques at will against any situation, if you are forced to do so.

FOUR OPPONENTS

1. Two opponents, one on each side, are grabbing each of your hands. Two more opponents are in front and behind you.

2. Execute the front kick to the opponent in front. With your left leg, you may aim at the opponent's midsection, while in an actual case, it may be more effective to deliver kicks to the opponent's groin or knee.

3. Bring down your left foot at the original position, and execute the right side-thrust kick to the opponent on your right.

4. To the opponent on your left, deliver another strong side-thrust kick.

5. With the same leg (the left leg in this case), deliver the strong back kick to the opponent in back. Again, in practice it is better to try to kick at the opponent's mid-section, but in a real situation, the kick should be focused on the opponent's groin.

DEFENSE AGAINST WEAPONS

AGAINST A THREAT BY A KNIFE: CASE A

1. Keep enough distance from the opponent so that the weapon would not touch you if the opponent extended his arm toward you. Look for an opening.

2. As you find an opening, execute the side-thrust kick to the knee of the opponent's front leg. This alone may incapacitate the opponent.

3. The opponent will lose his balance, but you should still maintain a distance.

4. Execute one more kick, this time the roundhouse kick to the opponent's head.

5. Jump in to grab the opponent's hand holding the knife.

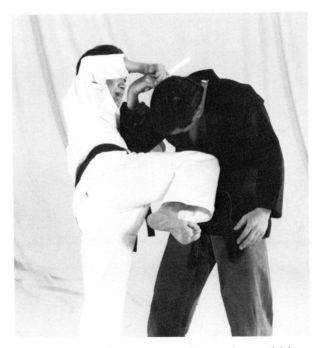

6. Twist back the opponent's arm by grabbing his wrist. To further weaken the opponent, if necessary, execute the roundhouse knee kick to the opponent's midsection. Take the knife away from the opponent whenever possible.

AGAINST A THREAT BY A KNIFE: CASE B

1. Carefully get close to the opponent.

2. Suddenly and quickly, execute the crescent kick to parry the opponent's hand holding the weapon.

3. Step in immediately and grab the opponent's hand holding the knife. Twist the wrist backward.

4. Take away the knife, as twisting the wrist makes the opponent powerless.

5. You can easily throw the opponent to his back by continuing the wrist-twisting technique.

AGAINST A THREAT BY A KNIFE: CASE C

1. As the opponent attempts to swing the knife in an up-and-down motion, step in swiftly and use the cross block to block the arm that holds the knife.

2. Immediately grab the arm that you have just blocked.

3. Deliver a strong elbow strike to freeze the opponent.

4. As the opponent becomes weak, start to execute a submission technique. You must be aware of the weapon at all times.

5. By pressing down the opponent's right elbow with your left forearm, as you place it on your right thigh, complete the submission technique.

6. Take away the weapon from the opponent as you continue the submission technique.

AGAINST A THREAT BY A KNIFE: CASE D

1. As you face an opponent with a knife, maintain a posture of confidence and concentration.

2. When you find an opportunity, suddenly and quickly execute the crescent kick to parry the opponent's hand holding the knife.

3. In a continuous motion with the same foot, execute the hard side-thrust kick to the opponent's knee.

4. Jump in to the opponent, and grab the arm that holds the knife. (It is good to take the weapon out of the opponent's hand whenever you can and as soon as possible.)

5. Twist the wrist of the hand that holds the knife, and throw the opponent backward. In an actual self-defense situation, you may employ any and every tactic available in order to overcome the adversary. A kick to the opponent's groin is one of the effective methods to weaken him.

1. In confronting an opponent with a knife, keep far enough away from the opponent so that the weapon cannot touch you if the opponent extends it toward you.

2. As you see an opening, quickly get close to the opponent and use the crescent kick to parry the hand with the knife.

3. With a continuous movement, spin back and pick up the other foot. Focus your eyes on the opponent over your shoulder.

4. Kick the opponent's temple with the hook kick. Follow this technique with a submission technique or take-down.

AGAINST A THREAT BY A GUN: CASE A

1. Suppose the opponent threatens you with a gun at the back of your head.

2. After showing no sign of resistance, with a sudden and quick motion, turn back and parry the opponent's hand holding the gun.

3. With a continuous motion, attack him with the other hand by executing the knife-hand strike to his temple. Keep grabbing the opponent's hand.

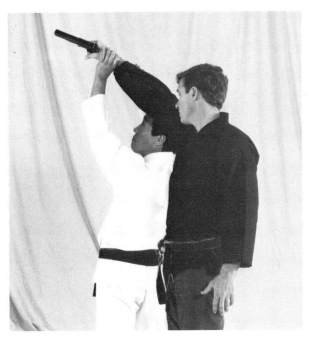 

4. After the freezing technique of the knife-hand strike, twist your body under the opponent's right arm and move to the outside of the opponent's body.

5. Execute the strong back kick to the opponent's groin.

6. Finish the self-defense with the submission. Place the opponent's right hand on your right knee and press the back of his elbow with your left forearm.

AGAINST A THREAT BY A GUN: CASE B

1. You are threatened by someone holding a gun at the back of your head.

2. With a strong and sudden motion, spin back to parry the arm that holds the gun.

3. Grab the hand that holds the gun.

4. With a continuous motion, execute the upper-elbow strike to the opponent's chin, while continuing to hold the opponent's hand holding the gun. At this moment, your right foot is placed in front of the opponent's right foot.

5. Bring your left foot all the way back to inside the opponent's left foot. Place the opponent's right arm on your right shoulder.

6. Using the springing power of the knees and the hips, in addition to pulling the opponent's arm over your right shoulder, throw him down on the ground.

7. You may finish the technique by punching or kicking the opponent on the ground.

8. If the opponent still holds the gun in his hand after the throw, take it away by pressing his elbow against your knee.

1. When threatened by a gun, stand still and concentrate on your abdominal power with quiet breathing.

2. Suddenly and quickly, parry the opponent's arm holding the gun.

3. With a continuous movement, execute a hard roundhouse kick to the opponent's temple.

AGAINST A THREAT BY A GUN: CASE D

1. Suppose that you are being threatened by a gun at the back of your head. Show no sign of resistance or fighting back.

2. Suddenly and quickly, turn back and parry the opponent's hand holding the gun.

3. Execute immediately the palm-heel strike to the opponent's philtrum as you keep holding the opponent's right arm.

4. Grab the opponent's right wrist, and twist it with both your hands as you turn your body under the opponent's right arm.

5. You are now ready to take the opponent down on his back by pressing on his right wrist.

6. Throw the opponent backward by pressing his right wrist, and take the gun as soon as possible.

AGAINST A THREAT BY A GUN: CASE E

1. When threatened by a gun at the back of your head, stand calmly and do not show any intention of resisting. Suddenly and quickly, turn back as you parry the hand that holds the gun.

2. Grab the hand that you have just parried and follow it with the elbow strike to the opponent's temple.

3. Place your left arm around and under the opponent's right arm, and push the arm down with your right hand.

4. Applying proper pressure to the opponent's right arm enables you to execute a standing submission of the opponent.

5. From the same position, apply more pressure to the opponent's right wrist by twisting it down. Retrieve the gun as soon as possible.

6. The final submission, if necessary, should be on the ground by pressing on the back of the opponent's right elbow and placing his right hand on your right thigh.

AGAINST A THREAT BY A GUN: CASE F

1. Suppose you are threatened by a gun from the right side.

2. With decisive movement, speed, and power, parry the opponent's arm.

3. With a continuous motion of your right hand, grab the opponent's hand holding the gun. Execute the left-elbow strike to the opponent's temple.

4. Once the opponent is weakened, take him down by twisting his elbow backward and applying pressure to his wrist.

AGAINST A THREAT BY A GUN: CASE G

1. If the opponent approaches you with a gun, stand without showing any intention of resisting.

2. Quickly use the high side kick from underneath to parry the opponent's hand holding the gun.

3. Immediately jump in to grab the opponent's hand holding the gun.

4. With the armlock, twist the opponent's arm backward. From this position, execute the outer major sweep.

1. If the opponent comes very close to you with a gun, stand without showing any intention of resisting him.

2. Suddenly, with a decisive movement, raise your right hand to parry the opponent's right hand (the hand holding the gun).

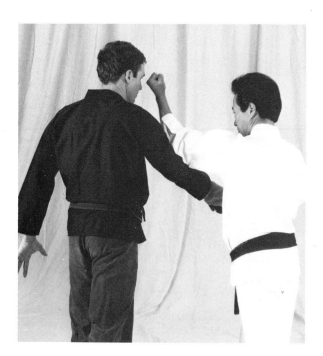

3. Grab the right arm, and follow it with a strong back-fist strike to the opponent's eye or the bridge of his nose.

4. As the opponent freezes from your back-fist strike, bend his arm backward. Keep control of the opponent's hand that holds the weapon.

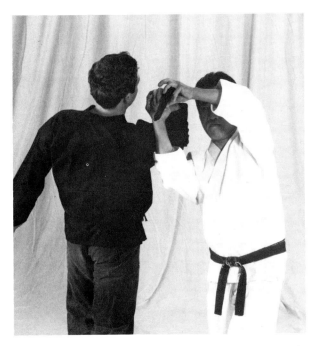

5. Bring your right hand under the opponent's right arm, and grab the opponent's right wrist. With your left hand, keep grabbing the opponent's right hand.

6. Take the opponent down to his back by twisting his right wrist. Take the gun as soon as possible.

FIGHTING SPIRIT

It is wise to live in peace with others and with yourself. If possible, avoid dangerous or potentially dangerous situations. But you may someday face a situation in which you are forced to defend yourself—with no chance of walking or running away from the opponent(s). If you cannot do anything to avoid the predicament and are forced to fight back, you must face the situation with resolve. Once you decide to defend yourself, you must do so *with no fear or hesitation*.

Imagine, for instance, that you are confronted with an opponent wielding a long, razor sharp sword. It is natural that anyone would become scared at such a moment. But you can overcome your opponent with strong willpower and determination. Your actions must be so decisive that you attack the opponent before he or she has had a chance to swing the sword down. You are bound to come out a winner.

You should be decisive in any fighting situation you are forced to contend with—and, in fact, in many other of life's circumstances. In making choices, accomplishing an important task, or playing a sport, decisiveness can give you the winning edge.

7 Kata: Theory, Demonstration, and Analysis

In the early days of karate, students had no sparring practice with which to develop their fighting ability. Rules for such practice had not yet been developed, nor was there proper safety equipment to protect students.

To help their students strengthen their fighting skills, ancient karate masters designed a system of formal exercises to be performed against imaginary opponents. In the view of many experts today, these prearranged exercises, known as *katas*, are the core of karate, for they best develop the individual's mind, spirit, and body.

At the physical level, kata exercises allow students to learn various blocks and attacks arranged so that they may be applied to real-life self-defense situations. Various shifting movements are included so that students can successfully take on up to eight opponents. Through continued practice, students develop muscle coordination, tone and strength, speed, balance, flexibility, and, depending on the energy and effort expanded, improved cardiovascular health.

Although *kata* is literally translated as "form," no kata is meant to be a static routine. Katas should be alive and dynamic, and students should practice each original pattern with their own expression and individuality—sacred and respected qualities to all karate masters.

At the mental and spiritual levels, kata helps to develop students' concentration, self-discipline, and patience. To foster this development, ancient karate masters made katas difficult to understand. By "hiding" the underlying techniques that could be applied to real-life situations, the masters encouraged students to meditate, or think through each movement and its application to real opponents.

Students had to discover gradually why each movement had been designed for a particular situation. Today, the formal analysis of kata, known as *bunkai* or *kai-seki*, helps students to learn how each technique can be applied to actual opponents. Karate instructors are schooled in this analysis and can tremendously help students' development.

In its most profound practice, kata, in fact, is seen as a form of *do-zen*, or moving meditation. Advanced katas indeed include abstract or symbolic movements and postures. Students who want to get the most out of katas should try to feel an esthetic sense of self-expression in each kata practiced and should concentrate on perfecting katas one by one. A student can boast of the number of katas performed but fail to *comprehend* the katas in all their fullness.

Although esthetic appreciation is important, students should never lose sight of the real fighting purpose behind the practice of kata. The battle against imagined opponents is serious—its conception often deadly—and the student really fights. Contrast this to a sporting sparring match, in which one real opponent scores against another in "imagined" fight.

In performing katas, students should keep the following elements in mind:

- ***Zan-shin* (the mind that remains alert)**—Mastery of kata includes developing a mind that is alert, calm, and ready to respond not only while techniques are executed, but also after the opponent has been defeated. While performing a kata, the student with zan-shin shows no opening to the opponent and finishes the fight perfectly, so that the opponent has no chance to recover.

Zan-shin allows one to spiritually and mentally dominate the opponent without arrogance, disorderliness, or weakness. Following combat, physical action is replaced with inner strength and calm.

- **Breath control**—Breathing is essential to life, and many ancient philosophies and practices place proper breathing at their core. Yoga, for example, teaches students to maintain mental and physical balance by linking of proper movement and breath control. Likewise, power, balance, and focus in katas are gained only through correct breathing.

  Generally you should inhale through the nose during preparatory and transitional movements, with the diaphragm pushed down so air is moved to the lower abdomen. Exhale through the mouth at the moment you execute the techniques, with the diaphragm pushed upward by forcing in the muscle of the lower stomach. Your shoulders should be relaxed during all breathing, making it easier to manipulate the diaphragm.

  As students progress, they learn to tailor the length of inhalation and exhalation (that is, short exhalation and short inhalation, long inhalation and short exhalation, and so on) to particular movements and body shifting. They also learn when it is appropriate to utter a breathing sound, and when not. The spoken or unspoken utterance of ki-ai—which is basically the exhalation of air through the abdomen at the moment of a technique's execution—adds power and focus to techniques and is absolutely inseparable from breathing.

- **Rhythm**—Correct breathing helps to maintain the rhythm proper to each kata and its meaning. Appropriate muscular intensity—sometimes powerful, sometimes relaxed—and comprehension of each kata movement also are essential. Spiritual and mental intensity, created by imagining real opponents, makes the kata come alive with the rhythm of music and life. A performance of kata by a truly accomplished master is inspiring in its appropriate power, speed, and, above all, rhythm.

- *Chaku-gan* (eye focus)—Primary comprehension of a kata includes knowing the number of imagined opponents faced, the directions from which they attack, and their methods of attack. The eyes of the performer must focus on the imagined opponent(s) at all times. Proper chaku-gan is essential for maintaining balance throughout the kata movements and transitions and is, in fact, a good test of the performer's understanding of the kata.

  At its deepest level, chaku-gan refers also to the mental and spiritual eyes that can "feel" an opponent and anticipate his or her next movement.

- **Balance**—In both the physical and mental sense, balance is crucial in any art or sport, and kata is no exception. Students should not worry if they lose their balance as they begin practice. But they must make proper balance—achieved by controlling the body's center of gravity in the tan-den—a primary goal of patient and diligent training. Loss of balance while performing kata completely weakens the effectiveness of technique, giving the imaginary opponent the opportunity for victory. Good balance implies control of the total self, which in turn means dominating the imaginary opponent.

- **Power and strength**—A good kata is a powerful kata, that is, one that is performed with all available strength. You should practice katas at your own pace and according to your ability. Older or physically handicapped persons, for instance, can modify a kata to perform it with their limited abilities and still draw great pleasure and inner strength from the experience. Ultimately, kata is a very personal expression of the self.

  In competition, of course, katas are performed as vigorously as possible with proper strength and power to win a good score from the judge. No one, however, should be impressed by a performer's *apparent* strength and power. Inconspicuous yet crucial muscle movements and breathing control are not obvious to casual observers, and only a well-trained practitioner or judge can appreciate these subtle strengths.

- **Gracefulness**—Gracefulness can be achieved only with a great deal of practice and training. The beauty of kata comes from a combination of all its qualities, and gracefulness reflects the refined comprehension of the meaning of kata's physical movements. Here, again, the expression of gracefulness is very personal and is achieved according to individual ability. In its most profound sense, a kata performance is a sacred self-expression that defies anyone's judgment.

  Let us look now at a demonstration and an analysis of kata. Washin-ryu ten no kata.

KATA DEMONSTRATION

There are many different katas in different styles of karate, each with special characteristics.

Washin-ryu ten no kata is one of the standard katas in this particular style. *Wa* ("harmony") *shin* ("truth") *ryu* ("style") *ten* ("heaven") *no* (" 's") *kata* ("form") can be literally translated as the "form of heaven." It is an important, basic kata that includes many basic techniques for blocks, attacks, stances, and body-shifting movements.

The major characteristic of this particular kata is that the performer moves very little from the origi-nal starting position; instead, the opponents come to the performer. A strong straddle stance is empha-sized where applied. A regular front stance and a straight front stance should be distinguished. Once you have learned the sequence and the meaning of each movement, try to perform the kata with rhythm.

To understand the meanings of the movements, please refer to the "analysis" (*bun-kai*) section (pages 274-288).

DEMONSTRATION OF
WASHIN-RYU TEN NO KATA

1. In the ready position with the natural stance, relax your shoulders, and feel power in your lower abdomen.

2. Keep your right foot un-moved, and move your left foot by turning it on the ball to face in the same direction as the right foot.

3. Bring your left hand to the right shoulder to prepare for the downward block.

4. Move your left foot forward, and execute the downward block with the left arm. The stance at this moment is the half-and-half stance ("immovable stance").

5. From the same position, by shifting your weight to the left leg, execute the right reverse punch to the opponent's midsection.

6. Shift the weight back to your right leg, and execute the left upper block.

7. From the same position, by shifting the weight back to the left leg and assuming the front stance, execute again the right-reverse punch.

8. Open your right hand to make the horizontal spear hand.

9. Place your open right hand with its palm side upward on the left fist. Place your hands in the middle of your chest. Bring your right foot forward, and form the modified cat stance as shown.

10. Move your right foot to the east to form the straddle stance. At the same time, execute the right knife-hand block.

11. From the same position, turn your eyes to the west and place your left fist on top of your right fist.

12. From the same stance, execute the double punch to the west.

13. Bring your left foot to the east, and let it rest on its ball. (The feet are parallel at this moment.)

14. Execute the side-thrust kick to the west.

15. Drop your left foot to form the parallel stance, and become aware of the opponent from the south.

16. Bring your right foot behind your left foot as you face the south. Place your right hand on top of the left hand with their backs touching each other.

17. Pivoting on your right foot, form the left front stance to the south as you execute the upper-cross block.

18. To the south, execute the right-hand back-fist strike as you step forward with your right foot. (Use the straight front stance at this moment.)

19. Turn to the north, and bring both hands to the right hip. (Your right hand is placed on top of the left hand.)

20. Move your left foot to the west as you turn to the north and form the front stance. Simultaneously execute the downward-cross block.

21. Bring your right foot to the east to form the straddle stance. (Your right foot must touch the left foot and then be brought straight to the side.)

22. After one second of pose, execute the right-hand roundhouse back-fist strike.

23. Bring your right hand back to your right hip.

24. From the same position, look to the west.

25. As you look to the east, place your right arm across your upper chest. Release your left arm at the same time.

26. Execute the right back-hand block to the east.

27. Maintain the same stance and execute the left-elbow attack to the east.

28. Follow the elbow strike with the right back-fist strike.

29. Look to the west and bring your left arm across the upper chest. At the same time, release your right arm.

30. With the same stance, execute the left back-hand block to the west.

31. Execute the right-elbow strike to the west.

32. Follow the elbow strike with the back-fist strike. At this time the hand must be brought at once inside the right arm.

33. As you execute the back-fist strike, maintain a good straddle stance.

34. Extend your left arm to the north, and prepare for the next move.

35. Execute the right-arm outside-inward block.

36. Bring your right fist to the middle of your chest with its palm side facing up.

37. With your right hand, execute the pushing punch to the north.

38. Execute the left outside-inward block.

39. Bring your left fist to the middle of your chest with its palm side facing up.

40. With your left hand, execute the pushing punch to the north.

41. From the same stance, cross your arms in front of your chest.

42. Execute the double downward block to the north.

43. From the same straddle stance execute the double inside-outward block.

44. Without moving your arms, bring your right foot to the west to touch your left foot.

45. As you form the cat stance by bringing your right foot forward and adjusting the left foot slightly, bring your hands to your hips.

46. From the same position, duck your head low.

47. Take one step forward with your right foot, simultaneously executing the double roundhouse back-fist strike (scissors strike).

48. Follow the scissors strike with the head thrust.

49. Raise your head and straighten your upper body.

50. As you look to the south, bring your left hand on top of the right hand.

51. Bring your left foot to the north, and let it rest on its ball. At the same time, execute the double punch to the south.

52. With your left foot, execute the side-thrust kick to the south.

53. As you drop your left foot on the floor after the side-thrust kick, assume the front stance and execute the right-reverse punch to the south.

54. Bring your right foot to the west slightly to form the strad-dle stance, and execute the left punch to the south.

55. Pivoting on your left foot, bring your right foot back to the south and form the natural stance. Bring your right fist to your left shoulder with its palm side up.

56. Execute the downward block with your right arm. Move slowly and deliberately.

57. Bring your left fist to your right shoulder with its palm side facing up.

58. Execute the left downward block with a slow and deliberate motion from the same natural stance.

59. Bring both arms in front of your chest with the palm sides of your fists facing in.

60. Execute the double downward block from the same natural stance. The motion is again slow and deliberate as you arrange your breathing quietly.

ANALYSIS OF WASHIN-RYU TEN NO KATA

The analysis of kata, or *bun-kai*, deals with the possible meaning of each movement of kata. By grasping the meaning of each movement, one can perform kata with more precision and feeling.

Bun-kai is not enough, because one must find possible applications and variations of applications as well. This is the reason why it is so important to find a good teacher and follow his or her instruction faithfully.

The following analysis includes the kata's movements of significant meaning.

PATIENCE AND EFFORT

Whether you wish to learn karate as a sport or for self-defense, a serious practice of karate will give you many benefits. It is an interesting and challenging sport, and it has become one of the most popular competitive sports worldwide. As a means for self-defense, karate has proved itself to be truly effective, if one trains diligently.

But since karate is a traditional art based on scientific principles, mastering it will require much effort. Also, if you continue to study this art, you will develop an ability to be patient. As you learn different techniques of karate, you will acquire patience by developing a sense of appreciation for the quality of effort needed to accomplish anything valuable in life.

Some people are athletically inclined from the beginning. They seem to absorb the physical aspect of karate faster than those who are not so physically oriented. In the long run, however, the athletic person does not necessarily achieve better results than the nonathletic participant. Experience has shown that, regardless of physical attributes, anyone who demonstrates patience and effort can make meaningful progress in karate. With a slight modification in techniques, karate has been taught to a group of mentally handicapped people as well as to physically disabled people. Karate does not discriminate in this sense, for all it requires of its participants is patience and effort.

AN ANALYSIS OF WASHIN-RYU TEN NO KATA

1. You are surrounded by four opponents. Take the natural stance, facing the north.

2. The first attack comes from the north, which you block with the left-arm downward block using the half-and-half stance.

3. Execute the right reverse punch to the mid-section of the opponent from the north.

4. The next attack comes from the north to your face. Block it with the left-arm upper block.

5. Execute the counter-attack to the opponent's midsection. The opponent blocks this attack and tries to grab your arm.

6. Twist your right wrist and remove the opponent's grabbing hand.

7. Stab the opponent's eye with the right spear hand.

8. As you assure the straddle stance, block the attack from the east, using the knife hand.

9. Grab the attacking arm, and execute the right side-thrust kick to the opponent's midsection.

10. As you drop your right foot on the ground after kicking to the side, use your right hand to execute the spear-hand strike to the opponent's eye. (This is not expressed in kata.)

11. Look to the west, and block the attack with the left-arm parrying motion. Grab the attacking arm immediately.

12. As you grab the attacking arm, execute the right-reverse punch to the opponent's face.

13. Execute the side-thrust kick to the opponent's midsection. (It could be a different opponent, of course.)

14. Drop the kicking foot on the ground, and bring the right foot behind it, crossing, to execute the stamping kick to the opponent's foot.

15. As you turn to the south, execute the upper-cross block with the front stance.

16. Grab the opponent's attacking hand, and, as the opponent tries to step back, follow him and execute the right back-fist strike to his face.

17. Turn to the north (the original front) and execute the downward-cross block against the front kick.

18. Grab the attacking leg, pressing its outer knee with your right hand.

19. Throw the opponent clockwise by pushing up with your left hand and pressing his outer knee with your right hand.

20. A different opponent comes from the same direction (the north) with the upper attack, which you block with the left knife-hand block.

21. Grab the attacking hand with your blocking hand.

22. As you keep holding the attacking hand, execute the right-hand roundhouse back-fist strike to the opponent's left temple.

23. A different opponent attacks from the east. Block with the back-hand block, using the straddle stance.

24. Execute the left front-elbow strike to the opponent's midsection with the front stance. Follow it with the right back-fist strike to the opponent's face.

25. Look to the opponent from the west, and block the attack with the left back-hand block.

26. Grab the attacking hand and execute the right front-elbow strike to the opponent's mid-section. Follow it with the left-fist strike to the opponent's face.

27. Execute the outside-inward block to the attack from the north.

28. With your blocking hand, execute the pushing punch to the opponent's solar plexus.

29. With your left hand, use the outside-inward block to block another attack from the north.

30. With the same hand, deliver the counterattack with the pushing punch to the opponent's solar plexus.

31. Execute the downward block to the kicking attack from the north. (In kata, you execute two downward blocks simultaneously, but in actuality, you are blocking two kicks consecutively.)

32. The opponent attempts to grab your neck. Parry to both sides with your two hands using the inside-outward block.

33. Pull back both hands to your sides. The opponent loses his balance a little when you pull your arms back.

34. Duck the opponent's attempt to grab your neck.

35. Execute the double-hand roundhouse back-fist strike to the opponent's ribs.

36. Follow the double-hand roundhouse back-fist strike with the head strike to the opponent's midsection.

37. Turn to the south and use your left arm to block the attack with the parrying motion.

38. As you grab the attacking hand, execute the right-reverse punch to the opponent's face.

39. Execute the side-thrust kick in the same direction. (Again, it could be a different opponent.)

40. Follow the side kick with the upper punch.

41. Execute the middle punch with your left hand.

8

Physical Conditioning Exercises

The art of self-defense does not require you to be superstrong physically to start with, although you will become quite fit physically as you continue training faithfully. To make your self-defense techniques most effective, you should be physically fit and strong—if not now, eventually. Some of the techniques involve sudden and powerful motions, while others involve a certain amount of agility. To perform those techniques, and for the sake of safe practice, you should engage in physical conditioning exercises before and after training.

In doing so, the most important thing is to keep your own pace, realizing what you can and cannot do. Try to progress gradually.

For example, the first exercises in this chapter are basic stretches. Some people can stretch their bodies more easily than others. The difference may be innate to a degree. However, if you do these stretching exercises correctly you should be able to achieve flexibility to a certain point. As with all the exercises, perform them gradually and consistently at your own pace. Don't try to become superflexible overnight.

Physical conditioning exercises not only improve your performance of practical self-defense techniques, they also make you feel better because you are in proper physical condition. After all, the es-

sence of self-defense includes an individual's total well-being in daily living, and if you are physically fit and mentally alert, the chances are that you can cope better with various situations. Self-defense, therefore, in the most profound sense of the word, includes overcoming obstacles and difficulties in life through self-discipline, self-respect, and concentration.

This chapter describes various exercises that will increase your agility, strength, coordination, stamina, and overall power if you faithfully continue to perform them. Of course, it is important not to overexercise before you practice techniques, lest you become too tired to learn them well. Basically, to loosen up for practice of the art of self-defense, you should concentrate on stimulating blood vessels for better circulation and nerves for balance and mental energy. Also, warm up each joint of the body properly so that it can function smoothly as you try different techniques.

Once again, it must be emphasized that each person should perform the exercises at his or her own pace. Some people may need to see a doctor before starting exercises such as ones described in this book. A periodic physical checkup is wise anyway.

PREPARATORY EXERCISES
WARM-UPS

1. Sit on the floor and grab one of your feet. Place the other leg in front of you.

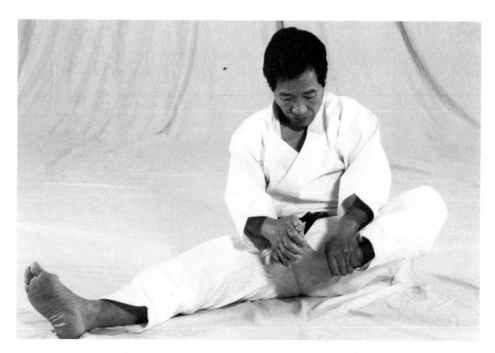

2. Rotate the ankle gently—never too fast or too hard.

3. From the sitting position, bend both knees to bring your feet together.

4. As you hold your feet together, push your knees down toward the floor. Also, from the same position, flex your knees up and down.

5. This exercise may be difficult for some people in the beginning. It loosens the thigh and hip.

6. From the same position, keep holding your feet and bending your knees completely, as you bring your head down to touch your toes with your forehead. Do it gradually and patiently.

KNEES—BENDING AND ROTATING

1. Stand with your feet together. Bend over and grab your knees.

2. Gently rotate your knees both ways.

FORWARD AND BACKWARD BEND

1. Standing with your feet together, bend forward until your knuckles touch the floor. Hold this position for a few seconds.

2. Keep your feet together, raise your arms, and stretch backward gently.

3. Slowly keep stretching backward. Do not force yourself too much in performing this exercise.

CONDITIONING EXERCISES

JUMPING OR WALKING IN PLACE

As you jump in place lightly, relax your shoulders. Light and low jumping is good for stimulating general circulation before actual workouts.

HIGH JUMPING

1. As you jump high, tuck your knees into your chest while you are in the air.

RUNNING OR SKIPPING ROPE

Running and skipping rope are good for those who wish to increase cardiovascular efficiency and strengthen legs. Depending on your pace and preference, two to three miles of jogging and about ten minutes of skipping rope are adequate.

2. As you jump high, stretch both legs to the sides while in the air.

Continued practice will strengthen the cardiovascular system, the legs, and feet.

ARM EXERCISE

1. Bend your elbows so that the heels of your palms are facing toward you.

2. Push out your hands with the feeling of striking the opponent with palm heels.

3. Push your hands upward with the feeling of pushing up something heavy above your head.

4. Push your hands downward with the feeling of pushing down the ground.

WRIST EXERCISE

1. Bend your wrists so that your palms face away from you.

2. Stretch your arms sideways with the fingers pointing inward as if your were holding something with the five fingers.

SWINGING AND PULLING ARMS

1. Stretch your arms to your sides.

2. Bring your arms in front.

3. While your arms are in front, make fists.

4. Pull back both arms to your sides. Repeat the whole sequence about 10 times.

SQUATS

Half Squat

1. Stand with your feet shoulder width apart. Stretch both arms in front.

2. Bend your knees halfway. Keep your back straight as you perform this exercise. Do not bounce as you bend your knees.

Deep Squat

1. Stand with your feet two shoulder widths apart.

2. Squat deeply with your back straight. Point your feet outward.

Light Squat

1. Stand with your feet together.

2. As you bend your knees lightly, press them against each other.

Full Squat

1. From the full-squat position, stand on the balls of your feet. Keep your balance with a straight back.

2. Lower your heels so that your feet are again flat. Relax your back and shoulders. Do not perform this exercise if you have a problem with your knees.

SIDE SWINGS

Gentle Side Swings

Relax your shoulders and arms, and swing your upper body, including the arms and the neck, lightly to each side.

Vigorous Side Swings

Swing your upper body with more power and speed. As you twist the upper body, your arms should be raised diagonally from your sides.

FORWARD AND BACKWARD BENDS

Backward Bends

1. Bend your upper body backward slightly.

2. Widen your stance to two shoulder widths. Bend your upper body backward deeply. Perform this exercise gradually.

Forward Bends with Feet Open

1. Bend your upper body forward slightly, with your feet wide apart.

2. Bend your upper body forward deeply. In this case, your head touches the ground.

Windmill Body Twist

1. Twist your upper body downward, and touch the fingers of one hand to the opposite foot. Try to hold the bending position for a few seconds.

2. Repeat with the opposite side.

Forward Bends with Feet Closed

1. Standing with your feet together, bend forward at the waist until your hands touch the floor. Perform this exercise gradually and at your own pace. Inhale deeply before bending, and exhale slowly as you bend forward.

2. Hold the bending position for a few seconds.

LOOSENING THE NECK

1. Stand straight with your shoulders relaxed. Keep your eyes open, and do not twist your neck too quickly when you perform this exercise.

2. Turn your face gently to the left.

3. Turn your face gently to the right.

4. Look up slowly with the feeling of touching the back of your head to your neck.

5. Tuck your chin down as you look down at your feet. To further loosen your neck, you may gently rotate the neck clockwise and counterclockwise.

LOOSENING SHOULDER TENSION

1. Pull one arm inward to your chest and hold the position for a few seconds.

2. Place the arm behind your head.

3. Push your head backward gradually and hold the position for a few seconds.

4. Repeat with the other arm.

FULL SQUAT AND FRONT KICK

1. Stand with your feet at shoulder width.

2. Bend your knees into a full squat. Keep your feet flat on the floor.

3. As you straighten your knees, stand on your left foot and kick with your right foot.

5. Repeat the same technique with the other side. As you come up, place your weight on the right foot and kick with the left foot. If you repeat this exercise for a certain length of time (say, for 30 seconds) with full speed and power, you will strengthen your cardiovascular system and the muscles of your legs.

4. As soon as you finish kicking, come down again to the full-squat position.

NECK STRENGTHENING

1. Lie down on your back. Bend your knees and place one of your hands behind your neck.

2. Push up your shoulders with your neck and feet. Repeat this exercise about 10 times before each practice. (Your hips will naturally rise as you push up the shoulders.)

ABDOMINAL EXERCISES

Minor Sit-Up

1. Lie down on your back and bend your knees. Come up enough to reach your knees with your hands.

2. From the same position, come up and twist your body to reach your left knee with both hands.

3. Then come up and twist your body to reach the right knee with both hands. Repeat 20 to 25 times for each direction.

Stretch and Tuck-In

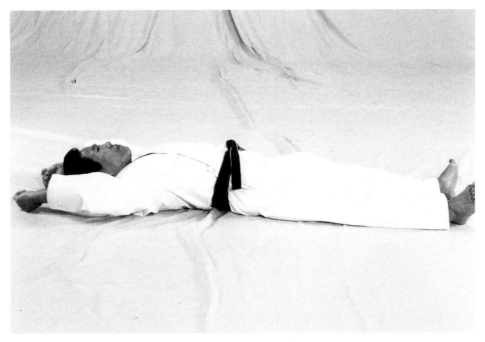

1. Lie down on your back. Straighten your legs and arms.

2. Raise your upper body, and bring your knees to the chest at the same time. Hold your legs tightly with your hands. Immediately lie down again. Repeat the routine 20 to 25 times.

Sit-Up

1. While lying down, bend your knees and place your hands above your head.

2. Raise your upper body without moving your feet at all. Repeat the sequence 25 to 50 times depending on your ability.

Double Leg Kick

1. From a sitting position on the floor, raise your legs. Keep your knees straight, and balance yourself with your hands.

2. Bend your knees and kick out with both feet. Repeat the sequence 15 to 20 times. It will strengthen your abdomen as well as your legs.

STRETCHING EXERCISES

PREPARATORY STRETCHING

Stage One

1. Stand with your feet wide apart. Place your weight on the left foot, and bend the left knee. Keep the right foot flat on the floor as you stretch the leg.

2. Place your weight on the right foot, and bend your right knee. Keep your left foot flat on the floor as you stretch the leg. Repeat to both sides gently in the beginning.

Stage Two

1. Keep your weight on the left foot, and keep the left knee bent. From this position, lift the left heel. This strengthens the ankle and the leg as a whole.

2. Keep your weight on the right foot, and keep the right knee bent. Lift the right heel. Repeat 10 to 15 times on each side.

Stage Three

1. From a wide-open stance, bend your left knee and keep the right knee straight. Your upper body should lean forward a little.

2. Bend your right knee and keep the left knee straight. Holding the position for a few seconds is more effective than bouncing.

STRETCHING

Stage One

1. From a wide-open stance, bend your left knee and keep the right knee straight. Leaning gently, reach for the left ankle with both hands and try to touch your head to your foot.

2. Bend your right knee and keep the left knee straight. Bring your head close to your right foot as you hold the foot with both hands.

Stage Two

1. Bend your left knee completely and keep your right knee straight. Stretch down until the right leg touches the floor horizontally. Lean forward slightly, and do not sit.

2. Bend your right knee completely and keep your left knee straight. Stretch down until the left leg touches the floor horizontally.

Stage Three

1. Sit on the floor with your legs open as wide as possible. Keep the knees straight.

2. As you exhale deeply, bend forward gently until your head touches the floor. Maintain this posture for a few seconds and repeat the stretch three or four times.

Stage Four

1. Keep your legs open wide and your knees straight. Gently twist your upper body to the right. Hold the final twisting position for a few seconds.

2. Twist your upper body to the left. Make sure that you keep your knees straight as you twist.

Stage Five

1. Sit on the floor with your left knee bent, keeping the right knee straight. Bring your head forward until it touches the floor. Perform this exercise gradually. Repeat the same exercise with the right knee bent, keeping the left knee straight.

2. Sit on the floor with your left knee bent and the right knee straight. Touch your head to the right leg. Repeat the same exercise with the right knee bent, keeping the left knee straight.

Stage Six

1. Sit on the floor with your left knee bent behind the hip, keeping the right knee straight. Bring your head down to the right leg, and hold this posture for a few seconds.

2. Sit on the floor with your left knee bent behind the hip, keeping the right knee straight. Bring your head forward until it touches the floor. Hold this posture for a few seconds.

Stage Seven

1. Keep your legs open as wide as possible and keep your knees straight. Push your head down to the right leg slowly, and hold the posture for a few seconds.

2. Bring your head to your left leg. Make sure that the right knee is straight as you bring the head down.

Stage Eight

1. Stretch the legs vertically, facing your right. Try to keep both knees straight. Bring your head slowly to the right leg, and hold the final posture for a few seconds.

2. Try to touch your head to your left leg. Exhale deeply and slowly as you try to stretch. Grab your ankle as you hold the final posture.

Stage Nine

1. Sit on your knees and lift your hips. Gently lean backward.

2. Perform this exercise in slow motion. If you have trouble with your knees or back, do not perform this exercise.

3. Keep leaning back until your head touches the ground. Hold the final posture for a couple of seconds. When you overdo this type of exercise, you may injure yourself, so use discretion.

Stage Ten

1. Sit on your knees and lift your hips. Lean gently to one side.

2. Hold the posture for a few seconds, then lean to the other side.

Stage Eleven

1. It is sometimes effective to use a ladder as an aid for stretching.

2. Stretch your legs from the front-kick position. Make sure that the supporting foot is flat on the floor.

3. Stretch your legs from the side-kick position.

4. Try to push the edge of your foot up and keep your upper body straight, instead of leaning away from the stretching leg.

5. Stretch your legs from the back-kick position.

6. Support your upper body by holding the knee of the supporting leg. Force your body to stay upright as much as possible.

PUSH-UPS
METHOD A

1. Put your feet together and place your knuckles so that the palm sides face inward.

2. This push-up helps to build up the biceps as well as the shoulders. Try to place your weight on the first two knuckles of each fist.

METHOD B

1. Put your feet together and place your knuckles so that the palm sides face each other.

2. Place your weight on the first two knuckles as you perform this push-up.

METHOD C

1. Push up with your feet together, keeping the fists next to each other.

2. This push-up emphasizes development of muscles in the upper chest area.

METHOD D: THREE-FINGER PUSH-UPS

1. Push up with your feet together and with the first two fingers of each hand pointing forward.

2. It is important not to perform these push-ups too fast.

METHOD E: ONE-FINGER PUSH-UPS

1. Try to place the entire weight on each thumb. Bend the arms slowly and stretch them gradually.

2. Do not perform these push-ups too fast. You may touch the knuckles of your index fingers as you come down. Note: This is not a necessary part of your training. It is shown here just for your reference.

METHOD F: JUMPING PUSH-UPS

1. Start with the regular form of push-up with the open hands.

2. After bending your elbows completely, push up the whole body into the air.

3. Clap your hands before you come down on the floor.

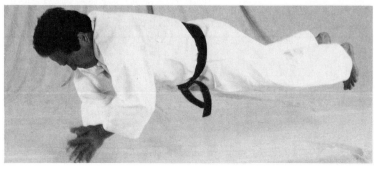

METHOD G: ONE-ARM PUSH-UPS

1. Push up with one arm, keeping your feet slightly apart. This type of push-up is not for everyone. Use your discretion in attempting them.

2. Place the other hand behind your back.

3. The farther apart you place your legs, the easier this exercise becomes.

METHOD H

1. Place your feet wide apart and place your hands on the floor, extending your arms and keeping your knees straight.

2. As you bend your arms, shift your weight forward. Try to keep your feet flat on the floor.

3. Keep pushing your body forward as you bend your arms completely. Stretch your arms as you arch your body, looking upward.

4. Come back to the original position. Repeat the whole sequence at your own pace.

STRENGTHENING LEGS

KICKING FROM THE GROUND: METHOD A

1. Lie on your back. Keep your right foot on the ground and kick with the left foot upward.

2. Keep your head above the floor. Push your right foot down as you kick with the left. Repeat the technique with the other foot, 10 to 25 times for each leg. Try a snapping motion as well as a thrusting one.

KICKING FROM THE GROUND: METHOD B

1. Lie on your back and kick out with one leg as you bring the other back.

2. Try kicking out with the toes pointed as well as with the heels out. Repeat 10 to 25 times for each leg.

KICKING FROM THE GROUND: METHOD C

1. Get on your hands and knees. Bend one knee, and kick away to the back.

2. Try to kick with your toes pointed and then with the feet flexed. Repeat 10 to 25 times for each leg.

KICKING FROM THE GROUND: METHOD D

1. Lie on your side on the floor. Tuck the kicking leg in tightly before kicking.

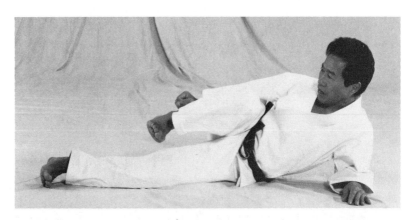

2. Kick to the side strongly with a thrusting motion. Curl up your toes and push out the side of your foot.

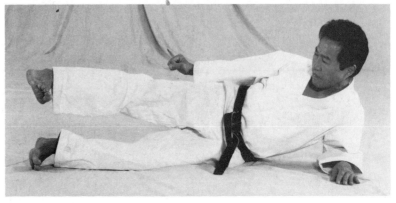

3. Kick up with a side snapping motion. Keep the outside of your foot up.

4. From the same position, kick forward with a snapping motion.

5. Repeat 10 to 25 times for each leg, depending on your level.

9   Karate and the Martial Arts: A Philosophy

The following essay represents my beliefs about the theory and philosophy of karate and is reprinted from my earlier book Living Karate.

Karate, etymologically, as a Japanese word that consists of two characters: *kara* and *te*. *Kara*, also pronounced "ku," means "empty." *Te* has the varied meanings of "hand," "method," "means," and even "trick." Therefore, the modern *karate-do* can be literally translated as "the way of the empty hand," *do* meaning "way" and/or "art."

In Okinawa, in addition to *te*, the word *to-te* had been used in some cases to denote the native Okinawan fighting art. To-te, also pronounced "kara-te," literally means "Chinese hand," since *to* (kara) is the name of a once prosperous Chinese dynasty (A.D. 618–907). When kara-te is expressed by the characters of to-te, it does not mean much more than the fighting art of Okinawa that had been much influenced by the Chinese fighting system. In this context, the concept of kara-te does not contain any spiritual or philosophical implications, although to-te undeniably included important spiritual and philosophical meanings in its teachings.

When the modern karate-do was officially introduced into the mainland of Japan in 1917 by Gichin Funakoshi of Shuri, Okinawa, it was decided that the word *kara* should have been expressed by "sky," instead of "Chinese." The two words have the same phonetic content but entirely different meanings. This change of the word added a profound meaning to the content of the modern art of karate.

The modern karate-do's kara connotes "emptiness," but it can also mean "sky," which symbolically refers to our universe or nature. Nature, as manifested by our universe, is all-encompassing and indivisible and recognizes no particular "friend" and no special "enemy." All are to exist and to be in oneness. Everybody is to be united as "one" under the universal principle. Kara also implies "absence of everything that is negative and destructive." This last meaning has a significant effect on the ethical foundation of modern karate-do.

In addition to the above-mentioned meanings, kara includes that of "emptiness of ego." Through the constant practice of the way of karate, a person should eventually be able to transcend the distorted ego, which is often the source of selfish and blind actions, so that his or her human relationships will improve with increased ability to create and maintain an atmosphere of harmony and peace.

One of the basic tenets of karate-do is that one should never make the first move in confrontation. This means, of course, that a karate student should never provoke or start any kind of physical violence. Only in absolute self-defense should one resort to the use of karate techniques. This principle of non-aggressiveness should not be taken as mere passivity or weakness. Rather, it means that a karate student should be equipped with a properly disciplined mind so that he or she can be aware of our constantly changing surroundings and cope with each situation according to "the Way."

Every once in a while, we hear of an instance where a karate student misuses his or her karate techniques to threaten or injure others physically. Needless to say, those who misuse karate techniques are not true karate students. They have learned only the superficial aspects of karate. They are interested in physical techniques alone and not in the total self-development of mind and body. It is interesting to see that each karate student seems to come to define karate differently, especially when an authentic teacher's guidance is not available.

It is akin to the situation of a blind person who touches an elephant's leg and is convinced that the animal is like a big tree trunk. Another blind person can have an entirely different opinion of what the elephant is by touching another part of the animal. The same thing can be said of karate. One student may consider karate a competitive tool, and for such a student tournaments are what it is all about. Still another student may consider the self-defense aspect of karate to be what the art is about, and this student may lose sight of other important aspects of karate.

Physical techniques in karate are surely important, since they express the principles of the art in a concrete way. As material phenomena, they can be viewed as a group of beautiful physical movements. Yet the true meaning of kara (*ku*) goes far beyond what these physical techniques can express. Let us now delve into the true meanings of ku.

Miyamoto Musashi, an extraordinary samurai who lived from 1584 to 1645, left a precious text entitled *A Book of Five Rings*. The last chapter of the book is called "The Book of Void" (or "Emptiness") in which Musashi explains the meanings of *ku* in the following way:

> . . . when the clouds of illusion [or "bewilderment" or "ignorance"] clear away, this is the true ku. In ku there is virtue [goodness], and no evil. Where there is wisdom, principle, and the Way, there is the true ku.

It is not difficult to see that Musashi's interpretation of ku is the same as that of the modern karate-do's ku in the ultimate sense. It is true that ku denotes nothingness and emptiness. But there is nothing negative in its meanings. Ku affirms everything and absorbs everything. At the same time, ku teaches us that the ostensible "reality" (what we perceive as real or true) should not be understood as the total expression of true reality. This understanding of ku enables one to recognize the importance of the sense of humility. A person who is truly enlightened in the art of karate is a humble one, because he or she lives with the meanings of ku. That person knows the limitations as well as the potential of the self as part of the great nature.

The importance of the true meanings of ku is such that one karate master in Okinawa used to call it *ku-te-do* instead of *kara-te-do*. This particular master truly lived in and with ku and really wanted to convey the ultimate meaning of his art to others, so he deliberately called it ku-te-do. It is regrettable that, as karate becomes more popular as a sport, somehow this meaning of ku seems to be less emphasized or learned by the students.

Now the *te* in karate includes various meanings. Its first basic meaning is the (biological) "hand," but in the more abstract and profound sense, it is a "means" and a "method." By understanding the true meanings of ku (kara), which should be viewed in a concrete way as well as in the abstract one, one should try to apply te in order to make the principle of ku work in the art of karate itself as well as in everyday life. The universe, in which we exist and of which we are part, includes the principles of ku and te. It is up to us human beings to understand and apply them to the fullest extent toward our total self-development and for the sake of social and individual well-being. Therefore, it can be safely said that the *te* of karate-do refers, in the ultimate sense, to that method by which we live most productively, constructively, peacefully, and in accordance with its inherent principles of the universe.

To actualize these profound meanings of karate-do, it is necessary for us to try to follow the long-established tradition of the art. The Way that our ancient master cultivated and maintained must be respected and learned, for it is the source of the wisdom of the art. At the same time, we must also realize that, as time passes, the social environments in which karate-do is practiced change. We should not become blind traditionalists, losing all proper sense of perspective. If we abide by the meanings of the true kara of the modern karate-do, we should understand that the Way must be in constant flux and cannot be rigid in form. Without altering its center, it must evolve so that it can direct and lead its follower to the right path. Therefore, the true kara (ku) is like water, which can assume the shape of any vessel, while blind traditionalism is like ice, so rigid and inflexible that it never conforms to anything other than its original shape. Traditionalism, if it gives any value to people, must be endowed with dynamic, living, and open spirit.

Karate-do, the modern martial art of empty-hand, can be defined as a system of self-defense that enables its students to develop their mental, physical, and spiritual potential to the fullest extent by providing physical techniques so that the student may become more aware of the self's relationship to the universal principle that is expressed in nature. Also, true karate-do comprises different elements so that it can be many things to many people, such as a method of self-defense, a sport (as a hobby or competitive game), a physical fitness program, a physical art of self-expression, and so on. Ideally, a karate student, under an enlightened teacher, should try to achieve a balanced view of the art of karate so that it can help to mold the whole person's character, although it is the student's prerogative to emphasize one particular aspect for personal satisfaction and benefit.

Karate-do, in its highest sense, is very similar to the meaning of *Tao* (the Way), which can be defined as the basis for all existence that flows naturally, existing in accordance with the laws of nature. Once understood in this light, the modern art of karate can be utilized effectively as a means for educating young people as well as a way of life for the more mature. It is important that we do not lose this perspective of karate-do, no matter what aspect of the art we may choose to emphasize in training, for it is the marrow of the art.

It has been said traditionally that there are three main groups of people who engage in the practice of martial arts in general. The first group consists of people who emphasize the spiritual side of the art more than anything else, constantly engaging in meditation but slightly neglecting actual physical training. The second type is the opposite: they believe in physical training and perfection of techniques to such an extent that they often forget that human beings are endowed with spiritual and mental qualities that can often become a major factor in determining the outcome of any serious physical encounter with an opponent. The third type of participants should be called "utilitarian" martial artists, because they believe that the most important thing in martial arts is to defeat the opponent(s) and that is all that counts. These people do not fully appreciate the philosophical aspects and the esthetic elements of the art. Needless to say, these approaches are all acceptable in a sense, each demonstrating one aspect of karate-do. But none of the above-mentioned extreme practices are truly representative of karate-do in the fullest sense of the word.

Since karate-do is a martial art (*budo*) and martial method, it can be utilized effectively in self-defense against violent attack, as has been discussed before. It can also be enjoyed as a sport and a method of physical fitness. However, the most essential meaning of modern karate-do is that of a martial art whose different aspects must be developed harmoniously. In other words, spiritual strength, mental power, technical proficiency, and overall physical strength must be developed simultaneously so that the greatest possible potential of the student is actualized. This balanced karate-do is a powerful and effective one in terms of self-defense, too. It is also meaningful for the sake of individual character development.

One of the important teachings among earlier masters was *Karate ni sente nashi*, which can be literally translated as "Karate does not include the first move (hand)." It means that one should neither make the first offensive move nor provoke violence. The principle of not initiating violence is not meant to convey mere passivity. In actual fighting or in a sport match, the karate student should be constantly alert to find or create an opening in his opponent's defense. A good offense is the best defense. The karate student must actively execute techniques when the time is right so that he or she can successfully attack the opponent. Karate ni sente nashi does not mean, therefore, just standing and waiting for something to happen. It is good to be able to respond to an emergency, but it is even better to be able to prevent the emergency from happening. This ability to prevent emergencies is desirable in the true karate student.

Interestingly, there is another important saying in karate that is ostensibly contradictory to the above-mentioned teaching. *Karate wa sente nari* can be literally translated to mean "Karate is the first move." It implies that one must be ahead of the other(s) in action at all times in order to achieve victory. Of course, this teaching may not necessarily concern the physical action, but the psychological factor that is involved in each situation.

If we understand the true meanings of the two seemingly different tenets, we immediately see that there is no contradiction between them. In fact, the two teachings are one and the same thing after all, expressed in different ways. The two tenets mean in essence that one has to execute self-discipline in daily conduct and never abuse the physical strength and techniques acquired through karate training, except in the case of absolute self-defense. At the same time, one must be alert enough not to give an opening, mentally and physically, to potential danger.

It is important, therefore, that you maintain an attitude of calmness and gentleness through which you seek harmony and peace among people. For the same purpose, you must be constantly active in creating a way of peace, in avoiding danger, in realizing the self's potential and possibility.

Among the most important words in martial arts are *sen-no-sen*, and *sen-sen-no-sen*. Sen simply means "ahead of" or "precede others," and it is the concept of reading the opponent's mind or intention and defeating the opponent by controlling his or her intended technique. As you face the opponent, who is ready to attack you, by summoning the spirit of sen, you attack the opponent one second before the opponent's action begins. In sen-no-sen, you let your opponent initiate his or her sen and defeat the opponent by preceding it with your technique. In other words, it is the sen that defeats the opponent's sen. In sen-sen-no-sen, you first let your opponent take his or her sen-no-sen against your sen, to which you react with another technique (or strategy) that controls and defeats the opponent's sen-no-sen. In other words, sen-sen-no-sen is sen that dominates and controls sen-no-sen.

Thus, the good karate practitioner is always ahead of the opponent so that he or she will not be defeated. Calm and yet constantly alert, the good karate student is like a good chess player who anticipates many future moves. For this reason, karate ni sente is at the same time karate wa sente nari. Thus, the two tenets are not contradictory at all; they are mutually inclusive.

There are other related concepts in martial arts that are also applicable to karate: *tsuki no kokoro* and *mizu no kokoro*. *Tsuki* means "the moon," while *mizu* means "water." Tsuki no kokoro can be literally translated as "mind of the moon." The moon that shines in the sky without prejudice, hatred, egocentrism, or a calculating mind can spread its light equally over all it can reach. It means that the karate student with this "mind of the moon" can be aware of the opponent's movement and intention; the student's mind is keen enough and clear enough to perceive everything that should be perceived regarding the opponent's mental attitude as well as the opponent's actual movements.

If, on the other hand, you are preoccupied by victory or defeat, fear of the opponent, hatred of the opponent, or even matters that have nothing to do with the opponent at the time, your mind cannot see clearly and correctly what the opponent is trying to do. This is akin to the moon that is clouded over and does not shine clearly and wholly. To achieve "mind of the moon" and attain proper techniques, you must train diligently according to the Way, with emphasis on meditation, as well as physically. Ultimately, this tsuki no kokoro must be applied to your daily life so that, in whatever business or work you are engaged, you can be effective and constructive.

The second and equally important concept is mizu no kokoro. Because mizu means "water," this concept can be literally translated as "mind of the water." The surface of water can be easily disturbed. A touch of the finger on its quiet surface suffices to make the whole surface of the water completely unquiet. Once disturbed, the water does not reflect correctly or in their totality the images of surrounding objects. Only when the surface of the water is undisturbed and clear does it reflect objects directly and correctly as true images. In the same fashion, the student equipped with the "mind of the water" can see the opponent clearly and directly, without distortion or self-deception; henceforth, he or she can deal with the opponent according to necessity and at will for the sake of the ultimate victory. The disturbed water's surface can be likened to a mind entertaining various thoughts, including the preoccupation with winning and losing, personal feelings toward the opponent, and others, some of which may not even have any relevance to the opponent he is facing.

This discussion of mizu no kokoro and tsuki no kokoro leads us to another important concept in martial arts that may be the highest state of one's trained mind. It is called *mu no kokoro* or *mu shin*. The kara of karate-do is akin to the meaning of *mu* in Zen. Mu literally means "nothingness" as well as "emptiness." Mu no kokoro or mu shin (*kokoro* and *shin* are the different phonetic expressions of the same word meaning "mind" and/or "spirit"), therefore, is the "mind of nothingness," the "mind with no thought," and the "mind with no conscious activity." If translated as such, however, it may connote something negative. But the mu no kokoro is in no way negative, and negativity has nothing to do with the mu no kokoro. On the contrary, it is the most active and all-embracing state of mind, that in which "unconscious consciousness" is working according to universal principles. It is the state of the mind that is totally in harmony with universal principles. In this frame of mind, you can accomplish whatever you mean to accomplish in a natural way, for it is the state of mind that knows intuitively what is right and what should be done in each situation, because it does not artificially (or logically) strive to know.

It is said in the teachings of Zen that, in order to see and to hear things in the truest sense of the words, you need this neutral mind with no conscious thought. The mind with no conscious thought is the mind devoid of conceptualization and logic. In this nonconceptual and thus error-free state, it is possible to experience the direct awareness of your being and the self's relationship with the universe. It is not antilogic, but it is above and beyond logic. Almost everyone has at least once experienced the insight that the most profound feeling is something that cannot be expressed in words. Words are not without value. They are important and even necessary in basic communications in the human world. But word-level is too superficial to convey the essence of the human soul, because it cannot go beyond the world of relativities. For this reason, in Zen, sense-intellect is not regarded as the final tool for knowing and attaining the truth.

Mu no kokoro or mu shin is like the mind of a child, free of difficult words or complicated experiences, a mind that sees, hears, and accepts all that surrounds the self just as it is, without distortions of language and logic.

Generally speaking, it may safely be said that the Western mind is logically and analytically oriented and, naturally, prone to difficulty in understanding and accepting the values and the meanings of the "mind without conceptualization." To complicate matters, this mu no kokoro cannot be understood through logic or analysis. The more you try to gain access to it through these means, the more inevitably it escapes. Your intuitive understanding is the only means to grasp it. Transcending words and concepts, it is through a sudden insight that you come to understand what it is. It has to be taken hold of, so to speak, by your whole being and cannot be simply theorized. To this end, you must submit to intensive mental and spiritual discipline, which is usually based on Zen meditation under a qualified teacher. It should be emphasized that meditation does not always have to be static and quiet. There is mediation in motion, called do-zen, *do* in this case meaning "moving *zen*." A certain kata practice in karate should be considered as do-zen, which is as important as *za-zen* ("sitting meditation") in the attainment of the "mind free of conceptualization."

A Zen practitioner uses words and logic, too, to a certain degree. But he or she sees the limit of such methods so clearly that their absurdity appears overwhelming. It is one of Zen's precepts that direct awareness and direct experience are interrelated. To clarify this point, consider the following example, which really happened. On an icy winter morning at a mountain Zen temple, a group of monks were washing their faces and hands around an outside well. One of their fellow monks came out a little late. Before he touched the water with his hands, he casually asked how cold the water was. Before anyone could answer his question, he was suddenly showered with the cold water by the master, who happened to be among the monks. The lesson was simple and direct: it was the best and surest way, and, as a matter of fact, the only way to know how cold the water was. The master did not say a word at the time, as he seldom did on any other occasion. Almost comical in retrospect, this incident was seemingly unimportant at the time. But the crucial meaning of the master's action becomes clearer as one reflects on its implication.

Let us now proceed to see how this mu no kokoro can actually work in the mind of an artist, for karate is an art, and its student is an artist in an ultimate sense. When asked what he was thinking at the time he created one of his masterpieces, a well-known painter answered, "I don't even realize that I am working when I am really working." In other words, in the highest phase of the mind, the painter is unconscious of what he is doing or, to put it another way, is not thinking of the fact that he is working. This is not a matter of mere concentration but goes far beyond it. The mind with no conscious thought, mu no kokoro, is at work within him. What he tries to describe, the object, and the one who tries to describe it, the subject, fuse in such a manner that the two become one. In that oneness, we see only harmony and balance. In the artist's work, the subject becomes the object and larger than life as it were. The spirit of the object dances on canvas together with the spirit of the artist.

When the artist sees the object that he intends to depict, and if at that moment the mind of no thought (mu shin) is working within him, he can penetrate the true essence of the object. In a sense, he can become the object itself. Conceptualized seeing is not true seeing. It is seeing through a veil of preconceptions and diverse thoughts, and it is not possible to see the true essence of the object by such means. Conceptualization, therefore, is a hindrance in "seeing" the object in the true sense of the word. It is only when you are completely free from it that you can see and grasp the object, and this is when you allow the object to "see" you in return.

The discussion of mu shin may be meaningless unless it is directly related to martial arts training. During fighting, whether it be a sporting situation or an instance of genuine self-defense on the street, if mu shin is effective, you immediately cease to worry about the consequences of the situation. Victory or defeat is no longer important, for the mind is being moved by "unconscious thought," and so-called mu prevails in your mind. Your whole movement and thought become completely harmonious with "necessity." In this state of mind, you can penetrate, although without consciousness, every part of the opponent—his or her legs, hands, and eyes, as explained in the discussion of tsuki no kokoro. Also, with this mind of unconsciousness, the expert karate practitioner can respond to any kind of techniques that are executed against him or her by the opponent(s), as explained in the discussion of mizu no kokoro.

Thus, the expert karate practitioner, who is equipped with mu shin, will somehow absorb the opponent's movement into his or her own movement, as a river with a strong current absorbs a weaker one to become a greater flow. It is all because of the universal principle at work in mu shin. For this reason, the accomplished karate practitioner can block and attack the opponent according to "necessity," which means that he or she does these things without conscious, reasoned effort. After the match, that person may not be able to remember how the match has been carried and how the victory has been earned.

When we use the term *martial arts*, the connotation is too often that of belligerence. Etymologically, the word *martial* comes from the Roman god of war, Mars, which may explain why general "martial" arts convey to the uninformed public an impression of violence. The Japanese word *budo* is normally translated as "martial art" or "martial way." The word *do* means, literally, the "way," and it can be translated as "art," too. But the point of focus should be the word *bu*. The ideogram *bu* consists of two characters, "weapons" and "stop." In other words, the original meaning of the word *bu* is "stopping the weapons," "stopping violence," and/or "stopping aggression." There is no concept of belligerence in it. From this viewpoint, it is clear that the true martial arts represent a way for cultivating mind and body so that each participant can become strong enough to live with inner peace as well as in peace with others. Thus, the true budo has a signification that encompasses both personal and social realms of human life.

Index